DATE DUE

DATE LOANED SLIP

Books due in two weeks from last date stamped below

WITHDRAWN
NDSU

a

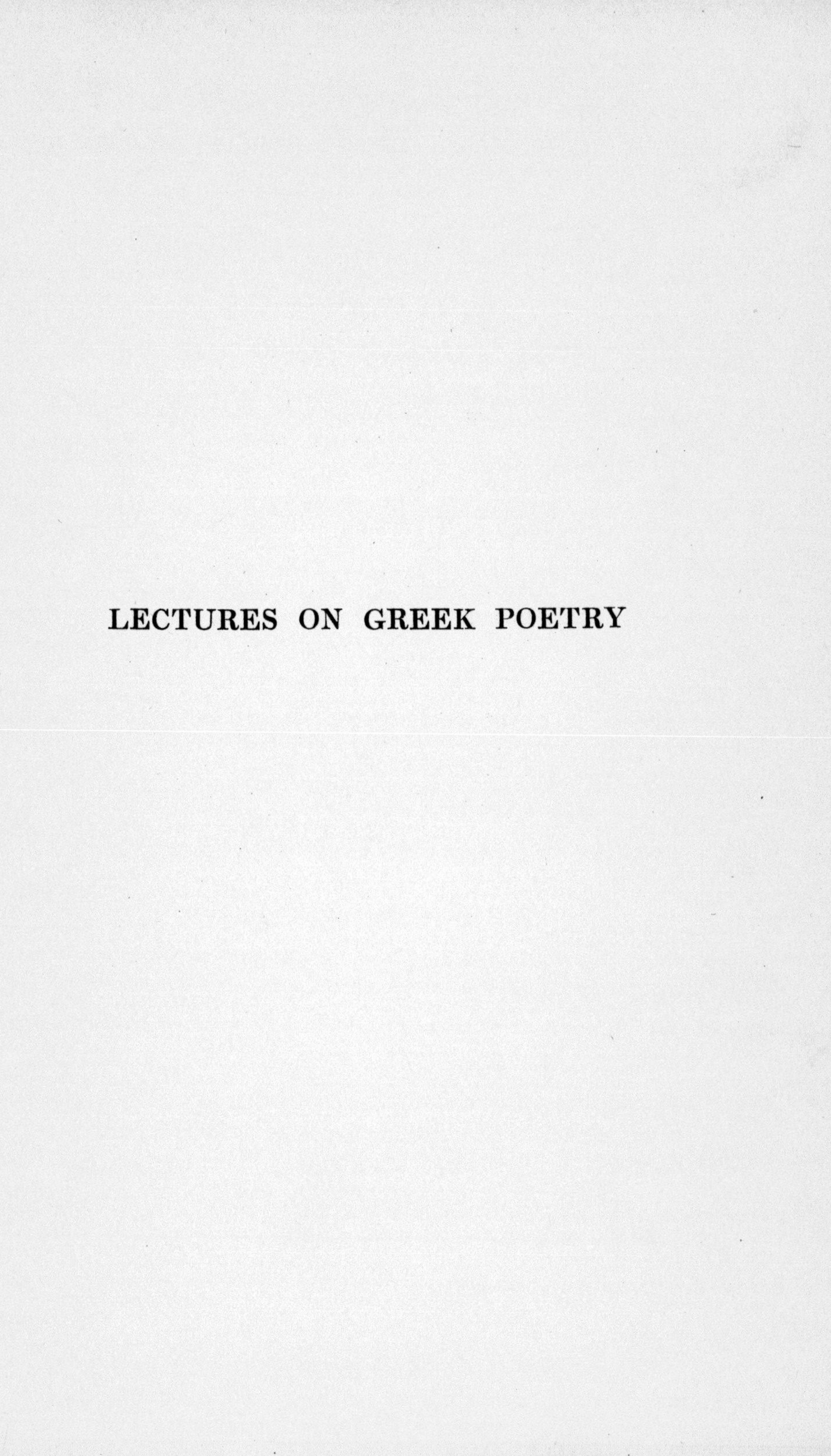

LECTURES ON GREEK POETRY

BY THE SAME AUTHOR

THE LIFE OF WILLIAM MORRIS. With 6 Photogravure Portraits and 16 other Illustrations. 2 vols. 8vo, 32s.

CHEAPER EDITION. With 2 Photogravure Portraits and 8 other Illustrations. 2 vols. large crown 8vo, 10s. net.

THE SPRINGS OF HELICON: A Study in the Progress of English Poetry from Chaucer to Milton. Crown 8vo, 4s. 6d. net.

SELECT EPIGRAMS FROM THE GREEK ANTHOLOGY. Edited, with Revised Text, Translation, Introduction, and Notes. 8vo, 14s. net.

POCKET EDITION, 2 vols. (Greek Text, 1 vol.) (English Translation, 1 vol.), fcap. 8vo, gilt top, each 2s. net; leather, 3s. net.

THE ECLOGUES AND GEORGICS OF VIRGIL. Translated from the Latin into English Prose. Square 16mo, 5s.

LONGMANS, GREEN AND CO.

LONDON, NEW YORK, BOMBAY, AND CALCUTTA

LECTURES ON GREEK POETRY

BY

J. W. MACKAIL

M.A., LL.D.

SOMETIME FELLOW OF BALLIOL COLLEGE
PROFESSOR OF POETRY IN THE UNIVERSITY OF OXFORD

LONGMANS, GREEN AND CO.
39 PATERNOSTER ROW, LONDON
NEW YORK, BOMBAY, AND CALCUTTA
1910

22562

All rights reserved

PA
3092
M3

O a new song, a free song.

Fresh and rosy red the sun is mounting high,
On floats the sea in distant blue careering through its channels,
On floats the wind over the breast of the sea setting in toward land,
The great steady wind from west or west-by-south,
Floating so buoyant with milk-white foam on the waters.

But I am not the sea nor the red sun,
I am not the wind with girlish laughter,
Not the immense wind which strengthens, not the wind which lashes,
Not the spirit that ever lashes its own body to terror and death,
But I am that which unseen comes and sings, sings, sings.

CONTENTS

INTRODUCTION

The lectures contained in this volume were given during the last four years from the Chair of Poetry in the University of Oxford. With these lectures is also now incorporated the substance of a paper read before the Classical Association at its General Meeting at Birmingham in October 1908.

While the lectures were planned in relation to one another as parts of a single continuous scheme, the circumstances of their delivery, at long intervals, and to an audience which (like poetry itself) is being perpetually renewed, implied a large amount of recapitulation and repetition. In revising them for publication, I have thought it best not to alter their form very materially in this respect; and I hope that the amount of repetition still left will not be found excessive, while it may serve to emphasise more effectively the central ideas by which I have been guided throughout, particularly as regards the poetical value of the Greek poets, and the way in which Greek poetry, as poetry, may best be read so as to disengage its living virtue.

Like the lectures on English poets already published last year under the title of *The Springs of Helicon*, this volume deals with one chapter in the larger and more comprehensive study of the Progress of Poetry. That study regards poetry, from first to last and in all its contemporary or successive incarnations, as a continuous function of life, of which it is at once an interpretation and a pattern. The pattern of life set before the world by Greece, the interpretation of life given by the Greek genius, are of unique value. To Greek poetry we owe our most vital knowledge of both, and in it both are most essentially and intimately embodied. It therefore requires, as it repays, the largest and most delicate appreciation. What I have tried to do in these lectures is to disengage its essence. By regarding it as it is concentrated in the work of a few great poets, I have sought to place its progress in a clearer perspective, and to bring it into a closer relation to life. To do this, on whatever scale, implies an amount of concentration and rejection which lays a heavy strain on a writer. His task is not on the one hand that of a historian of Greek literature, who sets out to give an account of the whole poetical product of Hellas so far as that is extant or recorded. Such a task is larger; it involves for its satisfactory performance not only wide and minute knowledge, but equally high gifts of insight, judgment, and proportion. Yet it is in a way easier, because its scope is defined; the problems are those of arrangement and handling rather than those of organic reconstruction. Nor on the other hand is the task that of a philosophic enquirer, "moving among ideas" and handling large abstractions. For there is no such thing as poetry in the abstract; and the study of poetry, while it deals with a continuous movement of the creative and interpretative imagination as applied to life, is only real in so far as it is a study of actual poems, and is only vital in so far as it keeps close to the great poets, to poetry at its highest power. To attain its object, it must not treat poetry either as a mere matter of history or as a kind of imperfectly expressed philosophy. It must regard and handle it as an interpretation and pattern of life.

In *The Springs of Helicon*, I dealt with the progress of poetry in England as, in the course of its evolution, it took shape in the work of three great poets, Chaucer, Spenser, and Milton. In these three poets, at long intervals, the movement of poetry became as it were visible and incarnate. Each absorbed into himself, and communicated to his own age, and to us, the effective integrated meaning of poetry as it had then been reached. The rest of English poetry, during the three centuries in question, places itself in relation to them. They supply key-notes, points of arrival and points of departure, for the whole of English poetry regarded as a continuous, progressive, and organic evolution.

This volume of lectures proceeds on a somewhat analogous method. It does not on the one hand make any attempt to give a general history of Greek poetry, or any complete review of the work of the Greek poets; nor on the other hand does it deal with its subject by abstraction and generalisation; and it treats of the poetical movement which was part of the life, and is still part of the vitalising force of Hellenism, mainly as that movement was embodied or manifested in the work of single poets.

In Greek poetry, as in the history of the Hellenic

civilisation itself, there are four main epochs. There is in the first place the mediaeval age, pre-Hellenic rather than actually Greek. Out of it the Greek world was born, and we know it as it reaches us through Greece. It is represented in poetry by the Iliad and Odyssey, the Hellenised Homer of a Homerised Hellas. The Homeric epic gives the pattern and interpretation of the life of that mediaeval world, as it took shape in the poetic imagination when it had already assumed the enchantment of distance, but still remained in some sense actual and alive. There is, next, the age of the creation of Hellas—of the purely Hellenic life, thought, art—interpreted in the terms of poetry by the lyrists of the seventh and sixth centuries. There is the age of Athens, the full Hellenic midday. Finally, there is the collapse of Hellenic life, and its reconstitution in new forms in a world saturated with Hellenism; and, in that age, the reconstitution of poetry among the Alexandrians before its central life passed from them to Rome and the West. Greek poetry did not then cease to exist; it continued a fitful vitality for many generations, and even as late as the tenth century of our era its faint notes may still be heard. But as an interpretative function of life it may be regarded as having completed its orbit by the time when the fresh Latin genius took up the torch from its weakened hands.

In the lectures on Homer which make up the first section of this volume, I have first given such a brief statement of what is known as the Homeric Question as was necessary in order to indicate, in its general lines, the view taken of the actual origin and nature of the Homeric epics. This was necessary to clear the ground for what follows, which is an essay towards the appreciation of the Iliad and Odyssey themselves poetically, simply as poems of the first rank. In dealing with the lyric age, I have concentrated attention on two poets: on Sappho as the greatest and most fully representative poet of the earlier lyric period, the age of freedom and expansion; and on Simonides as embodying the matured perfection of the lyric just at the moment when poetry was preparing to transmute itself into new forms, and pass under the ascendancy of Athens.

The central Athenian period, the age in poetry of the four great dramatists, is one which has been handled by modern critics and scholars with equal copiousness and ability. Its position may almost be taken for granted. Any history of Greek poetry, any work which purported to be a full study of the Greek poets, would necessarily deal with the Athenian dramatists as on the first plane of the canvas. It may seem strange that any volume of lectures on Greek poetry should omit Aeschylus and Euripides. But, for my own specific purpose, I have passed over both them and Aristophanes, as in *The Springs of Helicon* I passed over Shakespeare and the whole Elizabethan drama. To deal with them perfunctorily would be useless; to deal with them adequately would throw the whole scheme of the volume out of scale. But just as in the fifth century before Christ the whole life of Greek poetry was concentrated in Athens, so in Athenian poetry the specific Athenian achievement is to be found not in these other poets, but in Sophocles. The concentration of poetry has to be met by concentration of criticism. In a single lecture on Sophocles I have attempted to indicate, however slightly, the quality and value of his poetry as the full embodiment of the Athenian genius, just as Athens herself was the central embodiment of the genius of Hellenism.

Greek poetry, or such of it as is Greek in the full sense, is poetry after Homer; it is the poetry of a world in which, and for which, Homer effectively existed as a dominant influence. Even more fully we may say that the remainder of Greek poetry, from the year 406 B.C. onwards, is poetry after Athens. The main movement of this post-Athenian poetry took shape, after a long period of disintegration and diffusion, in the circle where the central figure, so far as there is any central figure, is that of Callimachus. Of this movement towards the reconstitution of poetry I have given a sketch in a lecture on the Alexandrians; and this is followed by studies of the two Alexandrian poets, Theocritus and Apollonius, in whom we may see most clearly the last interpretation of life effected by the Greek genius, and the premonitions of a new poetical world.

The position of Greek as a factor in culture has never been more assured than it is now. It moves beyond reach of the attacks of those who fancy themselves its opponents, and the alarmed outcries of those who profess themselves its only friends. It requires no elaborate system of artificial protection: it has become, in its own living virtue, part of our inheritance. Its study has increased and is increasing, both in width and in depth. It has ceased to rest on indolent tradition, or to be regarded as the appanage of a social class. It exercises over the whole modern world an influence astonishingly potent and pervasive. That influence is all the greater because it is no longer for us the expression of another world which, however fascinating, is yet remote from our own, but of a world brought by the expansion, liberation, and co-ordination of knowledge into close touch with the thought and art, the life and conduct, of the present day. The danger now is, not of Greek being studied too little, but of its study being on the one hand pursued too hastily and carelessly, and, on the other hand, distorted under the pressure of a specialisation which continually becomes more exacting in its demands. Against both dangers the safeguard is to be found in Greek poetry: for poetry will not be read carelessly; and it goes straight to the heart of life.

The aim of poetical criticism is to come nearer and nearer towards full appreciation, towards disengaging the essence of poetry. Attainment can at the best be only approximate: the horizon retreats before us. But it is just this which makes further advance always possible. The last word on poetry, or on any poet or poem, can never be said. If it were, we should have mastered the secret of life. But the next word is always waiting for some one to say it.

Our last word on poetry cannot be said; nor can our first discovery of poetry ever be remade. Yet it is just in so far as we can get near this double impossibility that the poets will bear to us their full meaning. Now and then at least, if we read poetry as it should be read, the reward will come, it may be with some great poem, it may be only with some passage or phrase, of entering fully and freshly into it, as though we read it for the first time and as though it gave the meaning of life. It is in such moments, "solemn and rare," that poetry performs its function for us—or rather, that we perform our function for poetry:

> To see a world in a grain of sand,
>   And a heaven in a wild flower,
> Hold infinity in the palm of your hand,
>   And eternity in an hour.

To attain these moments, no labour is wasted. To communicate them is the glory of the poets. To help towards their communication is the highest privilege, in their subsidiary province, of the exponents of poetry. For criticism is, or ought to be, the interpretation of poetry in some such sense as poetry is itself the interpretation of life.

Such interpretation is difficult; and nowhere more difficult than with those poets who have for many centuries been the schoolbooks of the civilised world, whose poetry only strikes home on us through thick layers of tradition, through the refracting medium of formal scholarship, through the distortion of what must always be imperfect understanding, not least so where we do not even know enough to realise the amount and kind of its imperfection. As we can only learn life by actually living, so we can only appreciate poetry by actually reading it ourselves, with our own eyes and our own imaginative effort; by our own appreciation, not by that of others. *Attingenda incerta ingeniis facta, alia vero ita multis prodita ut in fastidium sint adducta.* Much poetry is only obscured by the ingenuities of criticism: much ancient poetry—and indeed much modern poetry also—comes to us so overlaid by comment that its life can hardly strike through to ours. Any one who attempts a new interpretation, a fresh appreciation of it, must feel anxious lest he may be only standing between the poetry and the reader. And this is quite apart from the difficulties of his task as regards himself and his own appreciation. *Res ardua, vetustis novitatem dare, novis auctoritatem, obsoletis nitorem, obscuris lucem, fastiditis gratiam, dubiis fidem, omnibus vero naturam, et naturae suae omnia.* But the difficulty of the task does not make it less necessary. Such at least is the judgment of the University which, alone among those of the modern world, possesses and maintains a Chair of Poetry.

HOMER

A

I

THE HOMERIC QUESTION

THE Homeric question has been with us for more than a century, and while it has exercised and stimulated scholarship, it has also to some extent obscured Homer. For behind the Homeric question, and visible now only with some difficulty through the dust of controversy, lie the two things which really matter, the Iliad and the Odyssey. Nearly half a century has passed since Arnold, in his famous lectures on translating Homer, made a serious attempt to estimate the nature and the quality of the Iliad and the Odyssey as poetry. In such estimates there is no finality. Each age must make them anew for itself; but the time has now come when this attempt may at least be repeated in the light of a vast access of experience. During the last generation our knowledge of the ancient world, our methods of investigation, our armament of criticism, have all undergone immense expansion. We have reached a point at which it becomes possible to look about us, to sum up the results so far attained, and to set down certain things as either fixed or probable. Within the last few years, in particular, these results seem to have been clarifying and co-ordinating themselves. The work of specialists is being passed on to those who can use it critically and constructively. We still await some one to bring it together and vivify it, to give us back our Homer, enriched, understood, restored.

This has still to be done; and it will be done, we may hope with some confidence, within this or the next generation. The premonitions are too numerous to be ignored, too weighty to be neglected. My object for the present is partly to summarise, partly to anticipate. This is an almost necessary preliminary to any attempt at an appreciation of Homer. Without some indication of a point of view on the Homeric question, any discussion of Homer as poetry must be subject to ambiguities and misunderstandings. In doing this I merely propose to give a sketch or a suggestion of the position as it appears to me to stand now; to offer what seem to me results, without the processes by which they are reached, without proof or argument. This in any case is all that the occasion allows; and it is my apology for anything which follows that might seem, without this explanation, to be dogmatic. I shall be satisfied if I can suggest lines of thought, to be filled up or corrected by my readers from their own knowledge, and according to their own literary or historical, and above all according to their own poetical instinct. Much of what the modern Homeridae are concerned with does not enter into the scope of this sketch at all. I pass over their schemes and systems, some because they are already obsolete, others because they are for the present purpose irrelevant. I make no attempt to trace their history or to indicate the successive phases through which they have passed:

nor do I point the moral which forces itself on any one who casts his eye over that row of extinct theories, each once in its own time alive. They took colour, they drew their force and persuasiveness, from one or another master-theory prevalent, and accepted consciously or unconsciously, at the time; from some plausible "key to all poetries." It fed them with blood; as it ceased to do so, they also in turn faded back into bloodless ghosts, *νεκύων ἀμενηνὰ κάρηνα.* My object is now to consider the Iliad and Odyssey simply as two consummate achievements in poetry, from the point of view of one who considers poetry itself as a function, interpretation, and pattern of life. And as a preliminary to this consideration, it is essential, first, to regard the way in which Homer—using that word in its ordinary sense—came to be: and then, in the light of this process, to regard the effect of Homer on the genius and life of the Hellenic civilisation, and of the Hellenic civilisation on Homer. For Homer was before Hellas: yet Hellas gave us Homer.

In history, nothing begins and nothing ends: and it is not possible to assign any precise date to the birth of the Greek race or the Greek genius. They emerge from obscurity in a period of which we know little, and are not likely to know much more. For the knowledge that would be useful to us is not such as can be derived to any large extent from archaeological discoveries. These may often supplement, may sometimes suggest, but cannot create the substance of what it would be to our purpose to know. In sum, however, the main facts seem to stand somewhat thus.

Some time about 1100 B.C. the movement of peoples began which goes in ancient records by the name of the Dorian invasion. It broke into, and broke up, a mediaeval civilisation in the region afterwards known as Greece: that mediaeval, Homeric, or "Mycenaean" civilisation having itself succeeded, perhaps at a long interval, a still earlier and still more imposing civilisation of which the remains have yielded themselves to explorers in Crete. But that was a long, slow process; the Middle Ages, then as once again in Western Europe, died hard, or did not wholly die at all; they changed their life. For a full century—say from 1050 to 950 B.C. (such dates are mere convenient symbols)—there was a great tide of migration and expansion. The old Achaean settlements were broken up. The Asiatic coast was colonised from Europe. The loosely knit texture of the Achaean communities slowly transformed itself into a system of more definite monarchies and aristocracies. Beneath these, there began the first stirrings of self-conscious life among the people. The changes were not only material and external; they were not even only political or social. They were changes in the soul of man. The human mind took an advance of momentous importance; it gained a step which it has never since wholly lost. That step was the disengagement of the creative intelligence. Thought began; and with thought came the instrument of thought, letters. The alphabet was in general use by the end of the century of migrations; with the adoption of the alphabet, both as cause and effect, came the beginnings of Greek literature, and we may say, of Greek life.

The new age inherited a rich tradition of story and song from the mediaeval life out of which it had risen. When, reaching comparative settlement after a century of confusion and dislocation, it found in itself both the leisure and the capacity for art, it turned to those old inherited stories as to a world which had already taken on the enchantment of distance. The old Achaean, pre-Dorian world, still more or less familiar in its ways of life, as in its language and its dwelling-places, became idealised into an epic age. It was so idealised alike by its own descendants and by the Northern immigrants or conquerors who had mingled with them in blood and speech. This was so more especially on the Asiatic coast, where the fusion of the races was most complete. To these colonists, of whatever blood, came the appeal of a half-legendary past, with an overlordship of Argos and great deeds of a confederacy of princes. It came home to them all, as that of Arthur the Briton, of the Kingdom of Logres, and the feats of the Round Table, came home to English, Normans, and French, no less than to Britons, on both sides of the English Channel. The analogy is fertile in many ways; most strikingly of all in the way in which both these bodies of epic romance ignore history, ignore differences of race and severance of language, ignore even the cataclysms which separated that actual or imagined past from the present. We do not, for instance, look for, and we do not find, in the Arthurian literature any allusion to the Norman conquest of Great Britain. The literature and its whole environment are shut off from the world of the twelfth century, and from what lay historically behind that world, by an absolute barrier. There is no hint, no idea, that the mediaeval world had somehow been made, whether by slow changes or by violent shocks, out of the heroic Arthurian world; the question how the one thing was made out of the other does not even arise. So also it is with Homer. In both cases, too, the seed-ground of the new poetry is in a grouping of countries round a central sea; and that sea is not only a highway of commerce and migration, but the fluid medium (one might say) through which the movements of the human mind spread and communicated themselves so easily and so rapidly that they seem to arise simultaneously and independently in many different quarters. This is the important truth latent in a fertile remark of Coleridge's preserved by Scott: in Homer "there was, he said, the individuality of an age, but not of a country."[1]

Thus Achaean lays, traditionally transmitted, became the basis for both court and popular poetry. By 900 B.C., or thereabouts, we are in the age of the epic lays, the κλέα ἀνδρῶν. In both Iliad and Odyssey these earlier epic lays or *chansons de geste* have left unmistakable traces of their existence, and less certainly recoverable indications, now and then, of their actual form. The material of portions of the Iliad seems to have taken definite poetical shape on the

[1] *Journal*, under date 22nd April 1828.

mainland of Greece, in Thessaly or in Boeotia, at an early period in the century of the migrations—probably while the Peloponnesus was still Achaean. But all this is guess-work: the elaborate inverted pyramids of reconstruction that have been successively built up by theorising scholars go down at a touch. In the hands of their most brilliant exponents they seem to take shape for a moment, then dissolve and stream away into the mist out of which they rose. The epic lays were freely used by later poets; in some instances they were even, no doubt, incorporated *en bloc*, with but little change, in the new and larger structure. So far as they were already apt, they would not require readaptation. But the search after a primary Iliad and a primary Odyssey is in the main futile; so far as it is not, it is of little relevance. It is due to a deep-seated confusion between two things—a poem, and a story or stories—many of them already the subject of skilled poetical treatment—on which the poem was founded. "It is to the poet of the primary Iliad," says Jebb, "if to any one, that the name of Homer belongs." That sentence puts the fallacy in a succinct form. The answer to it is that there was no primary Iliad. So also, the saga which was the origin of the Odyssey probably took shape in Greece Proper before the migrations, or at least before its own migration; and that shape was poetry, though it was not Homeric poetry. It was not the "original Odyssey," any more than the saga summarised in Saxo Grammaticus is the original *Hamlet*. The argument against the unity of either

Iliad or Odyssey is in effect that which may be urged against the unity of any vital organism—

> Thou art not thyself,
> For thou exist'st on many a thousand grains
> That issue out of dust.[1]

The statement so often made, that "at least two poets have wrought" on this or that portion of the Iliad, generally amounts to no more than this, that the poet has there used at least two stories, at least two bodies of material, which lay before him in the work of two, or it may be of twenty, earlier poets.

By the beginning of the ninth century B.C. the epic lays, the κλέα ἀνδρῶν, had become a whole body of literature, in the full sense of that term. For them a literary vehicle, the Aeolian or mixed language, had been evolved and brought to high perfection; a metrical form of unsurpassed flexibility and beauty, the heroic hexameter, had been wrought out; their overwhelming vogue had, so far as can be judged, eclipsed all other poetical forms and subjects. The potentialities of epic poetry were created; the time was ripe for the great epic poet.

Then the great epic poet came. Somewhere on the Ionian coast or among the adjacent islands, in a sky sown thick with dust of stars, a great planet rose. Homer conceived and executed the Iliad.

That Iliad, in its main substance and its essential form, is the Iliad which we possess now. It passed through many vicissitudes. It suffered, as we shall see presently, one long eclipse or submergence. It

[1] *Measure for Measure*, iii. 1.

received accretions of substance, some of which probably are, some certainly are not, from the hand of its original author. Its dialectical forms were modified: in details it was retouched and modernised. But it remained the same poem. The canonical Iliad issued as an Authorised Version at Athens in the sixth century B.C., which is to all intents and purposes our Iliad, is also to all intents and purposes the original and only Iliad, the work of Homer.

About a generation—it may be as much as two generations—after the Iliad, the same poetical movement, the same quality of poetical genius, taking a fresh advance, produced the Odyssey. Speaking poetically, as a matter of art, the Odyssey implies the Iliad throughout. It is a work of lower poetical splendour but of higher technical skill. In this matter of technical skill the author of the Odyssey set himself, as it were, deliberately to excel the Iliad. The general tradition accepted through Greece later was that the poems were by the same poet, but separated by a considerable interval of years. This view is rejected by the overwhelming majority of modern scholars, but it cannot be said to be impossible. Even if we hold without hesitation that the Iliad and the Odyssey are by different poets—and it seems to me difficult to hold this without a good deal of hesitation—many of the arguments by which that view has been supported are either misstatements or irrelevances. Tests must be applied to criticism as much as to things criticised, and under these tests much of the destructive criticism of Homer loses its edge, much of the hypothetical reconstruction crumbles away. We must apply, here as elsewhere, the comparative method. There is no precise analogy; but the poet who produced the Iliad in the early prime of his life was, as one may put it, a poet capable of the artistic and poetical change which is felt in the Odyssey, among new surroundings, with an altered view of life, with an imaginative ardour burning less strongly, and with increased constructional mastery. As a masterpiece of construction the Odyssey is unsurpassed, perhaps unequalled in poetry. The tradition that it was the work of the advanced age of the poet of the Iliad is also in singular consonance with the fact that in the last books there may clearly be traced either a different or a failing hand. The last 624 lines were rejected by Alexandrian critics as a late addition. But there is more than that. Up to the nineteenth book the construction is masterly and the certainty of hand complete. From that point on to the end the constructive power flags; the workmanship becomes here and there hasty, unfinished, or uncertain. Whether this is due to failing powers in an aging poet, or to his death (as was the case with Virgil and the Aeneid) before he had finished his work, is mere conjecture; the author of the Odyssey may have finished (as Shakespeare does sometimes, and Scott habitually) in a hurry, or a pupil may have worked over and pieced out the master's unfinished conclusion. But in no case is the substantial unity of the Odyssey as a work of art affected.

Internal evidence, Jebb thought, was conclusive as to the workings of a different mind in the Iliad and Odyssey. A different mind may however come to a poet with the lapse of years and with fresh experiences. Analogies are slippery. But if we turn to the most Homeric of English poets, we shall find a different mind in the *Life and Death of Jason* and in the *Story of Sigurd the Volsung*. If we turn to Milton, we shall find, even at the interval of but a few years, the workings of a different mind in the *Paradise Lost* and the *Paradise Regained*, in form, technique, and substance. We shall find .in the *Paradise Regained* an analogous lessening of tension, an analogous shrinkage of similes, a different way (as is said of the Odyssey in contrast with the Iliad) of thinking of the Gods. We shall find that the vocabulary and syntax show marked changes. These changes are not only formal, but substantial. One instance will be sufficient to show what is meant as regards vocabulary. In the *Paradise Lost*, the "glass of Galileo," or the astronomer's "glaz'd optick tube" as it is called elsewhere, is referred to in terms which indicate it as something strange, unique, almost magical. In the *Paradise Regained*, the telescope and the microscope are spoken of by their ordinary names and quite as a matter of course. Were the methods of much Homeric criticism applied to Milton, this would be one of the facts cited to prove that the *Paradise Regained* belonged to a later cultural epoch than that of the *Paradise Lost*. Had the two poems reached us as the sole relics of a submerged world, subjected to all the subtle effects of changing dialect, of long transmission through imperfect manuscripts, of dispersion and re-collection, it would not be beyond the power of scholars to make out a plausible case both for a primary or "original" *Paradise Lost* and for the attribution of *Paradise Regained* to a different author belonging to a later generation.

So it is, too, with the Aeneid. With it we know the facts for certain. Virgil wrought up into it masses of older material; he left it incomplete at his death, full of variant readings, unfinished passages, unplaced episodes. It had to be arranged and edited by his executors. They did their work conscientiously and admirably; in particular, they scrupulously refrained from adding even a word anywhere. But even so, had the Aeneid reached us without any collateral or external evidence as to the circumstances of its composition, did we possess it as the earliest known product of Graeco-Roman poetry, reaching us out of an unknown world, rising like an island out of unplumbed seas, it would be easy to trace in it the work of different hands. There would almost certainly have been some plausible theory of a primary Aeneid, and of its expansion by successive insertions. At least three poets, other than the poet of the Italian epic which was the "original" or "primary" Aeneid, would have been confidently named as responsible for the third, fourth, and sixth books, besides a fourth who worked them over to make them fit into the poem as it took final shape. Whole passages would have been obelised. An earlier theory that it was made up by the skilful piecing together of a series of short poems would have been succeeded by a theory that an original core, to which large accretions had been made, had been wholly re-edited and re-shaped, and that the name of Virgil belonged, if to any one, to the author of the primary or Italian Aeneid.

By the end of the ninth century B.C. the Iliad and Odyssey existed: but Hellas did not yet exist. A century or more followed, the whole history of which is plunged in darkness. In literature, it is represented by the lost epics of the Cycle. Like the Chaucerians in England, the Cyclic poets carried on the Homeric tradition with continually dwindling powers: the record in both cases is one of swift decadence and growing incompetence; in both cases the last feeble efforts overlap the birth of a new poetry. A modern theory, urged with much learning and by some at least of its supporters with plausible persuasiveness, makes tradition invert the order of facts. It makes the Cycle consist of a mass of pre-Homeric epics. It represents it as the material out of which the Iliad and Odyssey were refined by a nobler morality and a more developed artistic sense. But the debasement of a style does not precede its culmination. As a matter of art, no less than as a matter of substance, the Cyclic epics imply Homer. They fell back, no doubt, on motives which Homer had deliberately rejected. This is what all decadent schools do, and reversion is inseparable from evolution. But no solid proof, no probability which commends itself as such to a trained poetical instinct, has been advanced against the consent of all tradition, that their object was to supplement Homer, that their method was to imitate him, and that where they struck out on a line of their own, they lacked the genius to succeed in it. The Cypria, written as an introduction to the Iliad, the Aethiopis, Iliupersis, and Nostoi, written to fill up the space between the Iliad and Odyssey, are dated early in the eighth century B.C. The stream of epic flows on from them in a fainter and fainter trickle, not wholly disappearing until the middle of the sixth century. Meanwhile, Hellas had been born.

In the dim records of the eighth century we can just trace the outlines of a life which was still pre-Hellenic, but which held in it the germ of Hellenism. The old kingdoms have mostly disappeared. Sybaris and Miletus are the two wealthiest and largest cities in the Greek world. Sparta and Athens are becoming important powers in Greece Proper. The afterglow of the mediaeval world, which had produced the age of the epic, had faded out; and on the eastern horizon appears, pale and clear, the dawn of a new day.

The earliest of the Greek lyrists, in whom the voice of Hellas first manifests itself, do not go back much beyond 700 B.C. Already by that time the memory of the Homeric poems had become faint. The Iliad and Odyssey, like two great mountain peaks, had retreated and become hidden behind the foot-hills of the Cycle. The life which they re-created and interpreted was very dim and remote. It is probable that their dialectical forms, and even to some extent their vocabulary, had become difficult. The new poetry, the poetry of Hellas, rose independently of them, except in so far as it was a distinct reaction from them, and except in so far as they had created a literary language which to a great extent remained that of the whole Greek world. The Greek genius had set itself to the two great creations which it introduced into the world and over which it spent its whole life—the creation of the state and the creation of the individual. The epic minstrels dwindled into court poets and became obsolete. For all the lyrists of the seventh and the earlier half of the sixth century, Homer might not have existed; we do not feel Homer in them.

In the sixth century begins the age of the democracies. It is then that Homer reappears. As the world travelled on, the foot-hills sank away, and in the broadening daylight the two great mountain peaks once more swam into the ken of Hellas. Homer had been brought to Sparta from Crete, we are told, nearly a century before lyric poetry was brought to Sparta direct by Tyrtaeus and Alcman. But, if so, he had not remained there as a vital influence—he had not struck root. The recitation of Homer was stopped, we are told again, at Sicyon by Cleisthenes about 600 B.C. Whatever this means, it means that Homer was no vital element in the life of Sicyon: it was like Justinian's closure of the Schools of Athens. The re-emergence of Homer, the launching of the Iliad and Odyssey upon the main current of Greek life, took place later. It took place at Athens in the time of Peisistratus. What Athens did for Homer, and what Homer did for Athens, we cannot say precisely; but we can say this largely, that Homer was the gift of

Athens, and Athens the gift of Homer, to Hellas and to the whole world.

In an age of few written texts and no exact scholarship, the Iliad and Odyssey had only survived, as it were, by a series of miracles. There had been much interpolation, much confusion, much cutting up; but the organic unity and organic life of the poems were so complete and so powerful that they had come through substantially intact. The text of the Odyssey, the various texts of the Iliad, which were collected by the enthusiasm and industry of Athenian scholars, enabled them to reinstate and give universal currency to an Iliad and Odyssey which were in substance the authentic Homer.

The term I have just used must be more closely defined if it is not to be misunderstood. The authentic Homer was not a fixed text. This is no paradox; it only seems paradoxical because we are so accustomed to poems which have assumed a fixed text—before the invention of printing as well as after—from the moment of publication. But when reading and writing were arts laboriously exercised and confined to a small number of skilled experts, there was no such thing as publication. A poet then retained his poem more in his own possession; he did more freely, more as a matter of course, what it is his natural tendency to do—remodelled, retouched, recast, rearranged, reworded, what still remained fluid and plastic in his hands. If he chose, this process only ended with his life. Even after that, it went on among those into whose hands the poem passed, so far as they were not restrained by reverence for the text as they had received it.

In the Odyssey, with its close-knit and masterly construction, little was likely to be done; even the conclusion, with all its imperfections, was accepted as it stood. The larger and more elastic scheme of the Iliad had admitted more variation and interpolation; it had paid the price also of its wider diffusion and its greater popularity. The work of the Athenian editors was clearly done with great judgment and with great conservatism. They may have carried further the Ionisation of the language which had been insensibly proceeding in the course of previous transmission. They were accused of having interpolated one or two lines; we can hardly doubt that they removed a considerable amount of accretions which had found their way into one or another of the texts which were before them. But they retained the Doloneia, which even according to the old tradition was a separate epic lay, written by the author of the Iliad, but not a part of the Iliad. They retained the additions, clearly post-Homeric, which had found their way into the account of the funeral games: they retained the so-called Little Aeneid of the twentieth book, which has all the appearance of an insertion that never became fully assimilated. But it is impossible to credit a late tradition that the Doloneia had not been inserted into the Iliad until then, and that, in the words of Eustathius, "Peisistratus added it." There is a vital difference, as all the members of the Society for the Protection of Ancient

Buildings are aware, between adding and refraining from removing an addition. Aristarchus at a later period obelised certain passages without removing them; that was a further refinement of editing. But what they left unremoved, the Athenian editors did not add, any more than Aristarchus added what he did not obelise. For the words "Peisistratus added this," we ought to substitute, "The Peisistratean editors found and accepted this addition."

Their work in main substance and effect was a reconstitution, to the best of their power, of the authentic Homer; and this was the Homer that they gave to Hellas and to future ages. When, three hundred years later, a fresh revision of the Iliad and Odyssey was made, the Alexandrian scholars did not, because they could not, go back behind the Athenian version. It was the Hellenic Homer. It issued from Athens, because Athens was already becoming the central focus of Hellenic art and life. But Athens became that, in great measure, through the Athenian capacity for appreciating Homer. If Athens in a sense made our Homer, Homer likewise in a sense made our Athens. Homer, says Plato in the *Republic*, has educated Greece—πεπαίδευκεν Ἑλλάδα. Athens, we may remember, had herself been called by Pericles the παίδευσις Ἑλλάδος, "the education of Greece." Both sayings are aspects of the same truth. Athens Hellenised Homer, and Homer through Athens moulded Hellas.

The effect of the re-emergence and dominance of Homer on the literature and life of the whole Greek world was swift and profound. From 500 B.C., or some years earlier, the whole of Greek literature implies Homer, is founded on Homer, is in organic connection with Homer throughout. Those great twin peaks dominate the whole landscape; their slopes feed the plains and cities of men with the produce of a hundred forests, the soil and water brought down by a thousand streams. The earlier Greek lyric, the flower of an age in which Homer was half forgotten, faded away or became transformed. The Attic drama was the creation of a Homerised Hellas with its Hellenised Homer. So, in varying measure, was the whole of classical Greek literature: not only the dramatists, not only the poets, but the orators, the historians, the philosophers.

Thus the touch of Homer upon Hellas had something of the same awakening and vivifying effect that the touch of Hellas has had, again and again, on other countries and later ages. The movement of the sixth century B.C., which brought Homer fully into the life of Hellas, was the first Renaissance. In the course of that movement the Homeric and the Hellenic genius were incorporated and became indissolubly one. Jointly they created what we mean by Greece; they created ideals towards which the human race has ever since turned its eyes. In that temple of the human spirit are ranged the Greek classics, the bronze and marble of fully developed Greek thought and art. Behind them the Iliad and Odyssey stand in the dusk of the inner sanctuary, like two statues in the ivory and gold of an earlier world. We measure and analyse them, we examine their chips and flaws, their rubbings and recolourings; we conjecture the elements out of which they grew, we try our best to reconstitute the world in which they were born; we please ourselves by tracing in them the work of successive hands and the accretions of successive ages. The Homeric question is always with us. But so is Homer; and to Homer we may now turn.

II

HOMER AND THE ILIAD

HOMER is but a name: and the Homeric poems, like the plays of Shakespeare, while they create a world, hardly reveal a personality. The Iliad and the Odyssey as they have descended to us show in each case the hand of a single great poet. But who that poet was, or when he lived, or how far he incorporated and how far he transmuted the work of his predecessors, we can only guess. Critical analysis and imaginative divination alike fail us when we come to the heart of the question. Still less can we form any notion of the poet's mind, of his own attitude towards the actual world in which he lived, or even towards the magical world which he presents to us. In both cases the personal note is as completely absent as it can possibly be from any piece of human workmanship. We seem to be looking on the work of some impersonal force, a *Deus absconditus.*

Shakespeare is so near our own time that we can almost reach back and touch him. We have his portrait, his signature, copies of his plays made in his own lifetime; we know all about the society in which he lived. No great cataclysm, no period of centuries whose history is dependent almost wholly on tradition or inference, separates him from us. A modern historian has not to say of him, as Herodotus says of Homer, "In my opinion he lived not more than four hundred years ago," and leave the subject there. We have records of his life, his christening and burial, his purchases and bequests, scraps of his conversation, a few rather coarse anecdotes. They all tell us nothing. When we say Shakespeare we mean the plays. But the plays answer none of our questions about their author. They are a mirror, and a mirror that has the strange power of making its own images: but it is nowhere transparent. Even his part in the plays is very uncertain. How much part had he in *Henry VI.*, in *Titus Andronicus*, in *Timon of Athens*? How far have any of the plays reached us as he wrote them? In *Henry VIII.*, and in several other plays, we have intricate and perhaps insoluble problems of mixed authorship: we can hardly be sure that we possess fully Shakespeare's own *Hamlet*, we can be almost sure that we do not possess fully Shakespeare's own *Macbeth*. And if this be true of his plays externally, it is still more true of them as revelations of a person. They do not tell us clearly, if they tell us at all, what he thought about life, the world, mankind. Except for merely external and formal allusions, neither the religious beliefs nor the religious controversies of his time might have existed for him. The contemptuous tone towards democracy which has been traced as a recurrent note in the plays is merely dramatic, and may be wholly artificial. For the actual Shakespeare, we have the key of the Sonnets—if we were sure how to fit it into the lock—and we have Shakespeare's women. But the Iliad and Odyssey rise before us, as they rose before the awakening consciousness of Hellas two thousand five hundred years ago, like islands out of an unplumbed sea.

From that same sea, long afterwards, through stages of which we can, with the modern armament of scholarship, dimly trace the rough outline, rose what we know as Greece, the Hellenic art, thought, life. The Iliad and Odyssey had, we may say confidently, assumed their form before then: before the Peisistratean recension, before the age of the earlier Greek lyric poets, before the beginning of authorised chronology. This assumption of form, which in the main issue made them what they are, was the work in each case of a certain poet of supreme genius. It is with the poems themselves, not with the material out of which they were shaped or the stages and processes of the shaping, that we have to do when we are considering poetry as a function of life. The earlier attempts to dissect either poem are now realised to have missed the main point. Later analysis, more skilful and better informed, has but little to do with the nature and progress of poetry. The Iliad and Odyssey are not rhapsodies in the obvious sense of that word, although they imply the work of rhapsodes. The complex product (this cannot be repeated too often) is analogous to a chemical rather than to a mechanical combination. But it is equally essential to remember that even the chemical analogy is far short of the truth. We have to do with life. Both poems are vital organisms, and their growth was organic, whether we regard it as the slow age-long deposit of some coral forest under the sea, or as the bursting into flower, in a single lifetime, of what had been long maturing invisibly in root and stem and bud. In either case they are the final transformation in the life and growth of a poetry which must have been living and growing for generations. The old careless view, due partly to ignorance and partly to misunderstanding of ambiguous terms, that they represent the birth of poetry in some fancied youth of the world, is as nearly as may be the reverse of the truth. They are not the birth of poetry; they are its full maturity, just before, in that particular form, poetry ceased to live and to interpret life. And the same is true of all the greatest poetry, as it is true, even more widely, of all the greatest art. Poetry itself, art itself, is indeed immortal. But its progress passes from one to another manifestation. We speak locally of sunrise and sunset, but over the world as a whole the sun is always rising and always setting. And when art fulfils itself, it is on the point of passing on elsewhither, of dismissing its finished task and seeking a new world to conquer and transform. For the age and country in which they came into being, the Iliad and Odyssey represent not sunrise but sunset, though to us, further towards the darkening west, *ποτὶ ζόφον ἠερόεντα*, they appear to be coloured with morning glories, to lie far off towards the sunrise and the dawn.

In one of the most profound and illuminating of his literary criticisms, Aristotle observes of tragedy that when, after passing through many phases, it had once fully realised itself, it stopped—ἐπαύσατο, ἐπεὶ ἔσχε τὴν αὑτῆς φύσιν. In the Iliad and Odyssey, as they assumed their final form, the epic "attained its nature." Then it stopped: there was nothing more to be done. Except for inconsiderable and one might say merely verbal alterations, the epic had crystallised in its permanent structure. Lines might be interpolated in a catalogue, or even a whole catalogue inserted; redundant passages might be added or removed; a large amount of verbal variation was a matter of course in a long poem transmitted only in manuscript, still more in a long poem mainly transmitted through memory, and habitually recited in fragments. Such a poem is still half-fluid, and no two copies of it are exactly alike. The text of Chaucer, or of *Piers Plowman*, shows us what can happen in such cases, and what is found to happen unless, as with the sacred books of the Jews, a literal sanctity was attached to the precise wording. It may be held as certain that the Athenian recension of the sixth century B.C. was no more than what it is reported to have been, a settlement of the text such as, three hundred years later, had to be made over again by Alexandrian scholars. The mere fact that it had to be made indicates in both cases that the poems themselves had been long in existence, and that the amount of local variation in their text was becoming excessive.

An analogous fallacy is the view, to which currency was given a century ago by the Romantic school, that the Homeric poems are "natural," in antithesis to Virgil for instance, or to Milton, who are "artificial." So far from the Iliad and Odyssey being natural epics, they are artificial in a very special and eminent degree. Those two islands rising out of unplumbed seas hold the salvage of a submerged continent. They have crowded into them all, out of a vast volume of poetry, that the Hellenic consciousness wished to save, or felt to be worth saving; or all, to put it in a different way, out of a dying world which refused to die, because it had in itself the energy of enduring life. It is in virtue of that immense energy that they are alive still. They contain dead matter, accidental accretions, or fragments of foreign bodies embedded in them without being fully assimilated; and it is in these that we find the main clues, scanty enough indeed, to the history of their growth. Of their origins we know in fact next to nothing. The national poetry of early Greece dealt, as early national poetry loves to deal, with a heroic period, compounded of history, imagination, and fable. It did not begin to take shape in epics until that period, so far as it had ever existed, was long over: it did not take final shape until a time in which the events it deals with were ceasing to be credible. This shape was final, partly because it was so satisfying that it could not be bettered, partly because the impulse of re-shaping had become exhausted, and interest and imagination began to move along other channels. We stand with regard to the Iliad and Odyssey somewhat as we should stand to Malory's *Morte d'Arthur*, if not only all Arthurian literature but all European literature previous to it had perished. Milton considered and rejected the Arthurian cycle for the subject of his epic. Far more impossible was it for Greek poets to melt up the Iliad and Odyssey and run them into new moulds. The epic had assumed stable equilibrium. The genius of poetry turned to the lyric, and the interest of poets to the new political life, the new individualism, the new thought, art, religion, which were beginning to stir throughout the Hellenic world.

On the first page of his collection of the Greek lyric poets, Bergk placed, with admirable insight, a fragment of two lines preserved by Pausanias from the work of Eumelus of Corinth. He was reckoned a poet of the epic cycle; and these lines are written in the Homeric hexameter; but in them the whole epic atmosphere has melted away. A new day has broken.

τῷ γὰρ Ἰθωμάτᾳ καταθύμιος ἔπλετο Μοῖσα
ἁ καθαρὰν κίθαριν καὶ ἐλεύθερα σάμβαλ' ἔχοισα.

"For to him of Ithome the Muse is well-pleasing that has a pure harp and free sandals"—the words take us out of the charmed Homeric air into the keen chill and sharp shadowless daylight of the Greek dawn. This was three hundred years before Herodotus: yet it seems separated from Homer by a still greater chasm of thought and tone. The speech of Polydamas, in a passage which the critics call a late insertion, seems to show the epic illusion disappearing before the same new impulse of Hellenic thought. The ideal Homeric world has been tried and found unsatisfying; mankind had to begin again. "In nowise wilt thou be able to take everything on thyself," says Polydamas; "to one God gives the works of war for his portion, to one the dance, to one viol and song; but in the heart of another Zeus the Far-Sounder lays excellent understanding, whereof many of mankind get profit: yes, and he saves many, and himself best knows it."[1]

ἀλλ' οὔ πως ἅμα πάντα δυνήσεαι αὐτὸς ἑλέσθαι·
ἄλλῳ μὲν γὰρ ἔδωκε θεὸς πολεμήια ἔργα,
ἄλλῳ δ' ὀρχηστύν, ἑτέρῳ κίθαριν καὶ ἀοιδήν·
ἄλλῳ δ' ἐν στήθεσσι τιθεῖ νόον εὐρύοπα Ζεὺς
ἐσθλόν, τοῦ δέ τε πολλοὶ ἐπαυρίσκοντ' ἄνθρωποι,
καί τε πολεῖς ἐσάωσε, μάλιστα δὲ καὐτὸς ἀνέγνω.

This, whether it be authentic Homer or not, is the full authentic voice of Greece.

By all probable analogy, which bears out, here as elsewhere, the fundamental soundness of tradition when tradition is not misinterpreted in order to support some irresponsible theory, the great poets from whose hands the Homeric epics were given to Greece and to the world lived just at the end of the times which were the Greek Middle Ages. Our habitual view of the Greek world as ancient partly blinds us to the fact that it was in all essentials intensely modern. They had had their Middle Ages, their centuries of feudalism, chivalry, romance, before the time when their recorded history and their extant literature (except so far as this is preserved in Homer) began.

[1] *Il.* xiii. 729–34. Mr. Leaf thinks l. 731 a tasteless interpolation. As to the epithet, opinions may differ.

Out of that mediaeval world, breaking it up and replacing it, there arose in Western Europe the nations, round the Aegean the city-states. There was an immense political upheaval, an immense expansion of colonisation and commerce; and behind both, and going deeper, a great liberation of thought, a great passion of freedom. The Iliad and Odyssey are the image which that modern world of Greece formed and kept of the mediaeval world that had preceded it. In this sense they are the first and one of the greatest achievements of the Greek genius; they are comparable to the work done, at the end of Greek life, by Aristotle. And just as Aristotle, at the time when the Greek city-state was perishing for ever, legislates for it in the *Politics*; just as Dante, at the time when the mediaeval Empire lay stricken to death, lives in a dream of it so intense that it almost creates from its own wreck the thing it contemplates; so there is little trace in Homer of the new Greek world. All three are completely absorbed in the story and spectacle of a great past, with no prevision of the future, hardly with any real appreciation of the present. That past was, as a matter of history, dead, if as a matter of history it had ever existed; but to them it was living, and through them it is still living to us.

The Icelandic genius, when it had perfected its epic, passed into romance. This seems a natural progress. It might, one fancies, have happened in Greece but for the invasion of new blood, life, and ideas—that is to say, but for all that we mean by Hellenism. As it was, the pure Greek mind was the least romantic of all in history. Hence perhaps the sudden and profound gap between Homer and the Greek poets. Some thirty years ago, Mr. Lang, in a fine sonnet, drew an imaginative analogy between Homer and the Nile. It is one full of suggestion. Out of trackless and apparently endless desert, the River descends into a land of which it is the highway and the life, which it fertilises and renders habitable. Its own life and growth are remote and unknown. Another modern poet has extended the analogy to poetry itself:—

Or I am like a stream that flows
Full of the cold springs that arose
  In morning lands, in distant hills;
  And down the plain my channel fills
With melting of forgotten snows.

Modern exploration has tracked the Nile to its source and mapped out its channel and its tributaries. The hidden course of that other stream we cannot retrace; it still issues in all its volume and splendour out of a land of mystery: *nec licuit populis parvum te, Homere, videre.*

That from the whole mass of pre-Hellenic poetry all that has survived is what was absorbed into the two epics of the Wrath of Achilles and the Return of Odysseus, is one of those things which for want of a better word we call accidental. Other episodes in the cycle of Troy offer equal scope for the poet. The return of Agamemnon supplied ample material for the greatest achievements of Attic tragedy, and the War of Troy after the Iliad became, still later, a treasure-house of subjects for romantic treatment. They are not in themselves less suited for epic handling than the two episodes actually chosen; and in point of fact the epic cycle dealt with them also, in the works attributed to Arctinus of Miletus, Lesches of Mitylene, Agias of Troezen. Nor was the epic confined to the Trojan cycle. From the Iliad itself it is clear that whole bodies of epic story quite apart from the tale of Troy were current, and had received the same large imaginative treatment: stories like those of Bellerophon and of Niobe, of the Quest of the Golden Fleece, of the Hunt of Calydon. But these two episodes, as it happened, were chosen and dealt with by a greater poet, and received at his hands an intenser poetical life. Nature, as science reminds us, produces life at equivalent cost of death; *nec ullam rem gigni patitur nisi morte adiuta aliena:* and the strong life of the Iliad and Odyssey swept into itself whole bodies of poetry, not epic alone, that were consumed in the process. It is this that gives them their unique richness. They are crowded with the treasure of a thousand wrecks. Like the Precious Shore in the legend of Britomartis, the ground is—

bestrowed all with rich array
Of pearls and precious stones of great assay,
And all the gravel mixt with golden ore.

Shortly upon that shore there heaped was
Exceeding riches, and all precious things,
The spoil of all the world; that it did pass
The wealth of th' East and pomp of Persian kings.

I spoke of Shakespeare's women as one of the two keys we possess to the real Shakespeare. Homer's women are likewise remarkable; yet one has the feeling throughout that they are only fragments, sparingly used and jealously scrutinised, of a lost world of poetry that may have held figures as great as those of Gudrun and Brynhild, of Imogen or Cleopatra. In the Iliad and Odyssey there are only two women in the foremost plane of the action, Andromache and Penelope. Both are vivid and actual, as fully alive as the men among whom they move; yet in both it seems as if the poet made them live almost against his will, or against the will of his audience; as though he would rather have given, or they would rather have had given them, generalised portraits of the faithful wife and affectionate mother. The recognition of Odysseus by Penelope might have been treated with the same power and tenderness as the parting of Andromache and Hector; is the Greek feeling about what was proper for women responsible for its being otherwise, and have the limits of the harder Hellenic taste lost for us one of the greatest passages in poetry? Even in the two great scenes into which Andromache enters, the parting in the sixth and the lamentation in the twenty-second book, may be seen or suspected a restraining force, un-Homeric in its origin, that makes us think mainly not of her, but of Hector. Hecuba, Cassandra, the strangely romantic figure of Briseis, mute except for her beautiful speech of lamentation over Patroclus, hardly count in the action. Arete, strong, gracious, capable, shows what the women of the Homeric world could be like if they were not kept subordinate. Calypso and Circe are witch-princesses, not human and not designed to be human, though the former at least shows touches of very human and very womanly feeling. One figure there is in the Odyssey never equalled except by the creator of Miranda and Rosalind, the girl-princess of Phaeacia. The poet sketched her in, largely, firmly, beautifully, and then stayed his hand. Perhaps no reader—certainly no modern reader—has not felt a pang of regret when she slips out of the story and out of our sight. Whether the poet felt that he had gone too far, that he had been carried away by the delight of creation beyond what the scheme of the Odyssey would bear; whether he was himself unconscious of the exquisite beauty of what he had created; whether, here as elsewhere, the hard, unromantic Greek temper refused to let the picture be completed, are questions which at once invite and baffle discussion: but Nausicaa disappears, and the sunlight seems to go out with her.

Through both the Iliad and Odyssey the figure of another woman moves in a sort of golden mist. Helen of Troy has already in them taken the place which is hers for all time, of one set beyond the bounds of mortality, a thing enskied, from whom a fire goes out that devours many, but on whom the fire cannot take hold. Her words over the body of Hector are the high-water mark of the Iliad; and it is not of Hector that they leave us thinking, but of her. Even in the domestic surroundings of her regained home in Lacedaemon she moves in the same unearthly calm, the white splendour of the Elysian plain which is destined for her final abiding-place, and whose atmosphere she carries about with her even on this earth. All voices, like those of the Trojan elders on the city wall, fall soft when they speak of her. Only from her own lips is any word of blame allowed to reach her. She is the one instance in which the romance of mediaeval Greece has been left in full play. Except with Helen, there is little in Homer of any feeling for women that we should call romantic, or even chivalrous. There is no morbid sentiment about them; but, on the other hand, there is the beginning of that harshness or chilliness which is a characteristic in developed Greek literature. It is one of the touches which make Patroclus different from all the other Achaean captains, that he had tried, clumsily perhaps, but affectionately, to make poor Briseis happy.[1] It sets him on the same plane with Hector. The perfect tact and courtesy of Odysseus to Nausicaa, when he first meets her, as again when he quietly parts from her, hardly touch the edge of chivalrous feeling; and in contrast with them we have his savage burst of anger at Melantho,[2] when he silences her by threatening to have her cut limb from limb—though no doubt she had provoked him beyond bearing and deserved all she got. But perhaps the most touching of all Homer's women is one obscure and unnamed; the poor maidservant in Ithaca who was weaker than the rest, and had to go on grinding all night to finish her task when the rest of her fellow-servants were asleep. There seems here a touch of something actual that had come to the poet himself and struck sharply through him the sense of

[1] *Il.* xix. 295–300.

[2] *Od.* xviii. 337–9.

the obscure labour and unsung pain that underlie the high pageant of life, war and adventure, the feats and feasts of princes. Perhaps in some Neleid palace, where at a banquet under the blaze of torches he had been singing to lords and ladies, like Demodocus in Phaeacia, of the glorious deeds of men, he had passed out of the darkened hall into the chill of morning; and there, while dawn was yellowing over Mount Latmus, heard a sharp peal of thunder across the Icarian sea, and then from the mill-house in the palace yard the voice of a tired woman over her quern: "They have loosened my knees with cruel toil to grind their barley meal: may this dinner be their last."[1]

On that island amid unsounded seas the waves washed up rough wreckage as well as treasure. Much of the fighting in the Iliad, or in such parts of the Iliad as appear to be extraneous to its essential scheme, is of this kind. But it is unsafe to argue that such passages are later accretions. Generally speaking, we cannot safely call any episode a later accretion which does not bear unmistakeable marks of lateness in its language. The author of the Iliad dealt prodigally with the whole material of the epic cycle, exulting in his riches, and confident, sometimes too much so, of the fusing and assimilating power of his own genius. But it is just this careless magnificence, guided by a lucid though not always a faultless instinct, that has given to the world in the Iliad what is probably on the whole the greatest poem ever made. Study of Homer from the point of view not of the scholar or commentator,

[1] *Od.* xx. 102–119.

but of the poet—that inarticulate poet whose presence in us makes us love poetry—shows one more and more that what is put in or left out is in nearly all cases put in or left out for valid poetical reasons. This is one of the chief rewards, let me parenthetically add, of the translator of Homer, whose work is otherwise apt to be so short-lived and, except for himself, of so little value.

While we may speak thus of the author of the Iliad, it is true also that the Iliad is the work of a whole nation. The nameless architect of Westminster Abbey, it has been finely said, was not this man or that, but the people of south-eastern England. Like a great mediaeval church, the Homeric poems embody the work of whole guilds of artists, of whole ages that appreciated art. In this sense the Iliad is a more artificial poem than the Aeneid or the *Paradise Lost*, as Westminster Abbey is than St. Paul's, because its origin was more complex, and its design lived and grew all the time it was being executed. The architect worked on a ground plan determined by existing building. He incorporated much of the earlier structure into his own work. Sometimes he pulled down and rebuilt, sometimes he remodelled into his own style or dialect without pulling down. For generations the masons were busy on the church, altering, extending, enriching. But the finished result thrills and burns throughout with the ardour of a continuous inspiration.

This ardour is what sets the Iliad apart from all other poetry. In the fine phrase of Dryden, Homer "sets you on fire all at once, and never intermits his heat." The notes of Homer given by Arnold, that he is rapid, plain, direct, noble, are all exactly true of the Iliad; but together with these qualities is another of at least equal importance, that the whole poem is at a white heat. Let me quote from a document now too little read, Pope's preface to his translation, that we may see how the Homeric ardour kindled an age which did not err on the side of over-enthusiasm. He is speaking of Homer's "invention," a technical term now obsolete, which bore much the same meaning as that which we now express by the term constructive or vital imagination.

"It is to the strength of this amazing invention we are to attribute that unequal fire and rapture which is so forcible in Homer, that no man of a true poetical spirit is master of himself while he reads him. Everything moves, everything lives, and is put in action; the reader is hurried out of himself by the force of the poet's imagination, and turns in one place to a hearer, in another to a spectator. The course of his verses resembles that of the army he describes—

οἱ δ' ἄρ' ἴσαν ὡσεί τε πυρὶ χθὼν πᾶσα νέμοιτο,

'they pour along like a fire that sweeps the whole earth before it.' Exact disposition, just thought, correct elocution, polished numbers, may have been found in a thousand; but this poetic fire in a very few. Even in works where all those are imperfect or neglected, this can overpower criticism, and make us admire even while we disapprove. Nay, where this appears, though attended with absurdities, it brightens all the rubbish about it, till we see nothing but its own splendour. This fire is discerned in Virgil, but discerned as through a glass, more shining than fierce, but everywhere equal and constant; in Milton it glows like a furnace kept up to an uncommon ardour by the force of art; in Shakespeare it strikes before we are aware, like an accidental fire from heaven; but in Homer, and in him only, it burns everywhere clearly, and everywhere irresistibly. This strong and ruling faculty was like a powerful star, which in the violence of its course drew all things within its vortex. It seemed not enough to have taken in the whole circle of arts, and the whole compass of nature, to supply his maxims and reflections; all the inward passions and affections of mankind, to furnish his characters; and all the outward forms and images of things for his descriptions; but wanting yet an ampler sphere to expatiate in, he opened a new and boundless walk for his imagination, and created a world."

Here for once the Iliad has been praised adequately, and one could wish that the passage were set to be learned by heart by all who approach the study of Homer. The fire of imagination lifts the height and swells the compass of a subject itself curiously contracted. The Wrath of Achilles is but an episode in a single war, as war itself is but an episode in the whole pageant of life. To this limit the subject of the Iliad is formally restricted in its opening lines; and lest we should lose sight of it, the restriction is as formally repeated in the speech of Zeus just before the crisis of the action, and emphasised still further by the magnificent image immediately following, of the far-travelled man whose mind ranges with the speed of thought over the whole length and breadth of the world.[1] Even good critics have stumbled here, and insisted that the action ought to be carried on to the death of Achilles. The author of the Iliad may be trusted to have known his own purpose; he certainly could not have stated it more clearly. And indeed it is obvious, if one takes the pains to think the matter out, that the action stops exactly where it should, and that to continue further would have thrown the whole poem out of scale. Doubtless it might have pleased Homer to choose a better subject than that of the Iliad, or at least a different one; but it is equally certain that it did not please him to do so.

The Wrath burns in a world which it transforms into fire. Nowhere else, except in Dante, does fire so penetrate the whole structure of a poem. It is perpetually present in single phrases or elaborated descriptions; fire blazing in a forest, fire licking up the plain and scorching the river, fire signalling from a besieged town, fire flashing out of heaven, fire leaping on a city of men while the houses crumble away in the roaring furnace, the fire blazing round the head of Achilles by the trenches, the fire that streams all night from the burning of Patroclus, the constant sense of the day coming when holy Troy itself will flare up in the great doom's image. Idomeneus in his richly chased armour is "like in his strength to fire." The Trojan host follows Hector

[1] *Il.* xv. 49–77, 80–2.

"even as flame." "Like flame," Hector leads them on. In a splendid reduplication of phrase he declares his resolve to face Achilles, "yes, even though his hands are as fire, though his hands are as fire and his might as flaming iron." Four times over the full fury of battle is summed up in one intense line, "Thus they fought in the body of blazing fire." The curtain falls on the slaking of the burning for Hector, "as far as the strength of the fire had gone," with flame-bright wine under the kindling fires of dawn.

The whole Iliad moves in this element of intense ardour. Ordinary life is going on its course all the while, but we only catch glimpses of it. The description at the end of Book VII. of the chaffering in the Achaean camp between the soldiers and the provision ships from Lemnos gives briefly but vividly enough a picture of the traffic of the everyday world going on alongside of the tragedies of kingdoms and the feats of heroes. Domestic life is absent from the main action except where, as in the Hector and Andromache episode, it is seen lit up by the lurid light of war. The allusions to it are chiefly in similes, so used as to bring the action into relation with an opener, a wider and less intense life. They are like the little bits of lovely rural or domestic background in old Italian pictures. Such are the vignettes of the poor spinning-woman and her children (xii. 433–5), and of the boys harrying the wasps' nest (xvi. 259–62); or the many pictures drawn from the life of the herdsman or sailor, the hunter, or smith, or ploughman. One of the most remarkable is that (v. 770–1) of the man sitting, like a Theocritean shepherd, on a cliff-top and gazing over the purple sea to where the horizon melts in haze. The largest and most highly finished is the set of scenes portrayed on the shield of Achilles. They give a picture of the whole world—a world wider than that of the Iliad, or even than that of the Odyssey, inasmuch as it includes the whole of ordinary human life. There were wrought the earth, and sky, and sea; the unwearying sun and filling moon and all the stars; cities of men in peace and war, with their weddings, feasts, and lawsuits, their raids and sieges and battles; ploughing and reaping and vintage, river-meadows and hill-pastures, tillage and hunting. All that *Heimskringla*, that round world encircled by the outer seas, lies in cool daylight; the fighting is not a strife of heroes "mixed with auxiliar gods"; the Ocean-river is not bordered by the groves of Persephone or approached from a witch's island; there is no word of the purpose of God being fulfilled through woes innumerable, or of destruction being spun for men that there might be a song for times to come.

In the main action of the Iliad the supernatural element is felt everywhere: it even shapes and colours the physical background. It is a land of thunder and earthquakes, of God-haunted mountains and seas. Twice over the sky drizzles blood. The plain of Troy is like an amphitheatre ringed round with awful faces. Before the city with its God-built walls, swept by the winds of the world, gods charge down upon one another in the mêlée, or sit apart watching the battle. From their cloud-capped towers, Zeus on Ida and

Poseidon on Samothrace look down into the arena. Silver-shod goddesses rise, like a mist, out of the grey sea. Lemnos is the home not only of the merchants who supply the camp, but of Sleep, the brother of Death. On the crest of Ida, hidden in a golden cloud that the sun cannot pierce, is a marvellous sub-tropical paradise, where the dew-drenched lotus, crocus, hyacinth do not merely, as in Milton's cool Eden, "with rich inlay broider the ground," but rush out of the divine earth.

Over this scene passes, too often for us to regard it as accidental, a mystery of darkness. Night, of which as a half-personified Power Zeus himself stands in awe, descends upon and involves the action. In the cooler atmosphere of the Odyssey night is for sleep, or at most for telling tales in the hall of a king's house, or sheltered in a swineherd's cottage from the wintry wind and driving rain. The cresset borne by Athena in the hall at Ithaca to light it up for the moving of the armour is magical, but with no natural magic. But much of the action in the Iliad is heightened by this sense of natural magic where it takes place in the dark: the troubled council in the Achaean camp and the embassy of Phoenix; the Doloneia, with its perilous night journey, where the thick-muffled silence is broken by the cry of the unseen heron; the coming of the Winds from Thrace to blow all night round the pyre of Patroclus and sink with the sinking flame just before dawn; the visit of Priam to the camp and his return with Hector's body. Even daylight is often obscured by strange mists and supernatural darkness, that now aid and now hinder flight, within which men struggle blindly and unseen. "Thus fought they," about the corpse of Patroclus, "in the body of fire, nor would you say that either sun or moon yet endured, for in that battle all the captains were wrapt in mist, while over the rest of the field warriors fought in clear air and sharp sunlight, and not a cloud was seen on the land or on the hills." From that "affliction of darkness and battle" rose the prayer of Aias: "O our Father, save us from the darkness; give sight to our eyes, and in the light destroy us if thou wilt."[1]

On this lurid shifting background, now incredibly clear, now wrapped in a pall of darkness, the action burns. The waves of battle surge backward and forward across the plain. Kings and stately women look on from the battlements of the city. Among the dense ranks of spearmen the princes, like knights at Creçy or Roosebek, move ponderously along the fighting line. They are heavily sheathed in bronze plate-armour, with huge crests and immense leathern bronze-clamped pavises, "like towers," reaching from neck to heel. They tilt at one another with long fifteen-foot spears, with sword and mace and battle-axe. Helenus swings a huge Thracian sword, like Durindana or Morglay, that shears away head and head-piece. From behind the knights' pavises the archers, crouching "like a child by its mother," rain their arrows. Teucer, like Einar in Olaf Tryggvesson's last battle, shoots from the side of Aias, striking down man after

[1] *Il.* xvii. 366–73, 645–7.

man, until his bowstring breaks, and he betakes himself to his heavy armour and long bronze-headed spear. The clatter of weapons on plated helms and cheek-pieces resounds like an armourer's forge. Huge stones are hurled as if from perrières by knights who have lost their spears; where one hits, a prince crashes down with a rattle of armour, "like a tower amid the throng of fight." Above all the clash and din rise the voices of the captains, men of great stature and prodigious strength. Some fight in armour splendidly damascened in gold or silver and inlaid with enamel. Achilles can run at full speed in all his battle-gear, a feat like those told of Richard Cœur de Lion. Aias wields a thirty-foot pike at the defence of the ships. "As when winter torrents flow down the mountains to a watersmeet and join their raging floods through the deep ravine;" "as when angry winds shaking a deep wood in the mountain dells clash and shatter the long boughs," so they fight; "and the iron roaring went up to the vault of heaven through the unharvested sky."[1] Here and there, while winged arrows leap from the bowstring and stones clash upon shields, a mailed figure lies still amid the whirl of dust, great and fallen greatly, his feats of knighthood forgotten, in the sleep of bronze. Behind on both sides rises the clatter of chariots and the continuous shouting of the massed soldiery, close-ranked with shield locked in shield: "the sound of the two hosts went up to the firmament and the splendours of God."[2]

Such is the world of the Iliad, set before us with

[1] *Il.* iv. 452–5, xvi. 765–9, xvii. 424, 5.

[2] *Il.* xiii. 837.

incomparable fire and splendour by the genius of a great poet; a world as brilliantly coloured as that of Froissart, as tense and vivid as that of Shakespeare. If we ask what relation it has to reality, we raise the whole question of the relation of art to life. The Homeric world is a world imagined by Homer. It is placed in a past time, evidently thought of as distant, though there are no exact marks of chronology any more than there are in the *Morte d'Arthur*. The destruction of the Achaean rampart, after Troy had been left desolate, is a thing long accomplished; "so were Poseidon and Apollo to do in the aftertime."[1] Helen in the Iliad, Alcinous in the Odyssey, speak of the whole war of Troy as ordained for a theme for poets of a remote future. But it was not so distant as to be wholly alien from actual life; it was not uninteresting or unintelligible to the poet's audience.

The life of a nation is partly to be sought in the mirror held up to it by its national poetry. But it has another and larger side. In the Iliad, as in Froissart, we hear little of the common people who were to become the nation of the future, and nothing at all of the gathering forces which were to sweep away the mediaeval world of romance and chivalry as the nine days' torrential rain swept away the Achaean rampart and laid the sand smooth on the beach. The professional minstrel or guild of minstrels is not concerned with common life. The common people in the Odyssey, the "princely swineherd," Eurycleia the nurse, Melanthius and Melantho, all the rest upon

[1] *Il.* xii. 34.

the crowded living canvas, are only studied in their relation to the principal figures; they are an enriched background. In the Iliad, but for the single burlesqued figure of Thersites, there are none. Whether the Homeric poems took shape at some feudal court like that of the Neleids of Miletus, or in later and more fully Hellenised surroundings, they are in essence court poetry, adapted to the taste of a court, or of a public which took its taste from that of a court. For the under side of that brilliant tapestry we have to turn to Hesiod.

III

THE HOMERIC EPIC

THERE seems no reason to discard the tradition which makes the two bodies of poetry passing under the names of Homer and Hesiod about contemporary. Whatever amount of recasting took place from time to time in the manual known as the *Works and Days*, or, as the title might be more aptly translated, the Farmer's Calendar, the life it sets before us is substantially that of the time in which the Homeric poems were produced. The world dealt with in the epic is going on somewhere overhead, unintelligibly, only felt by common people through the added pressure of misery that it brings upon them. "The son of Cronus now and then," says the rustic poet, "destroys a broad army or a wall, or takes vengeance on their ships in the sea"—

ἄλλοτε δ' αὖτε
ἢ τῶνγε στράτον εὐρὺν ἀπώλεσεν ἢ ὅγε τεῖχος
ἢ νέας ἐν πόντῳ Κρονίδης ἀποτίνυται αὐτῶν.[1]

This is to him, and to the people from whom he sprang and to whom he belongs, the whole upshot of the Iliad and the Odyssey. Hesiod's picture of life, vivid and detailed as it is, has no beauty. The life he

[1] *W. and D.*, 245–7.

knows is "hidden," obscure and laborious: κρύψαντες γὰρ ἔχουσι θεοὶ βίον ἀνθρώποισιν.[1] It is the wrong side of the pattern of the round world portrayed on the shield of Achilles, the subterranean crypt of that splendid church with its soaring columns and traceried vaultings, its organ-music and window-fires. The difference of subject and treatment is sharply given in two phrases: Homer sings of the κλέα ἀνδρῶν, the feats of heroes, Hesiod of the ἔργα ἀνθρώπων, the industries of men. If the Iliad is the *Morte d'Arthur*, the *Works and Days* is the *Biblia Pauperum* of early Hellas. In the rare passages where Hesiod rises into the epic tone, it is with a difference of accent and intention that makes his language less like Homer's than like that of the Hebrew prophets who were the first voice of the democracy. The men of the bronze age, he says, went down nameless into the pit, and terrible as they were, death took hold upon them.

καὶ τοὶ μὲν χείρεσσιν ὕπο σφετέρῃσι δαμέντες
βῆσαν ἐς εὐρώεντα δόμον κρυεροῦ 'Αίδαο
νώνυμνοι· θάνατος δὲ καὶ ἐκπάγλους περ ἐόντας
εἷλε μέλας, λαμπρὸν δ' ἔλιπον φάος ἠελίοιο.

The tone and even the very wording of this remarkable passage are just those of Isaiah in one of his grim dirges of awful exultation over fallen kings and kingdoms.[2] In a later age, the heroes of Thebes and Troy perished in "wicked war," no longer spoken of in the epic phrase as "man-ennobling." The Odyssey gives us

[1] *W. and D.*, 42. [2] *W. and D.*, 152–5; *cf.* Isaiah xiv. 4–23.

a flash of this lower world, working itself up painfully through the dark, in those famous lines where the ghost of Achilles desires, if only he might be alive, to belong to it, to be a day-labourer on the farm of a poor man like Perses of Ascra. It is a world of hard work and hunger—*αἴθοπα λιμόν*, "flame-bright hunger," as Hesiod calls it,[1] in one of those curious phrases taken from the court poets and made, half in innocence, half in satire, into an awkward ornament. The voice of the people was still inarticulate; it halted and stammered. The epic diction is used in a timid, laboured way, as the only known means of expression for any continuous or considered statement. So, too, the virtues inculcated are those of hard work, secrecy, thrift; they are virtues imposed by necessity, not freely chosen. The large epic generosity is for those whose generosity costs them little. The tales of poets are for the rich, who can afford to waste their time listening to them. In certain things—in a kind of close humorous observation of nature, and in the recognition of the passion of love between men and women as one of the large forces in life for good or evil—the Hesiodic poetry preserves elements which the epic at some time or other had deliberately discarded, though they have left traces of their presence. Of the two, Hesiod is much the more religious. On one side his religion bears the original meaning of that word; it is formal, cramping, superstitious; on another it reaches deeper than anything in Homer. For with Homer the Gods are almost part of the scenery; the moral government

[1] *W. and D.*, 363.

of the universe is a dim background expressed under symbols like the Weirds, the Vengeances, the Prayers, the Watching; the real divinity is the unconquerable mind of man. Homeric religion is that of a governing class, simple, and not deep. If the result is that much in Homer is frankly irreligious, on the other hand there is no great national poem so free from superstition, or in which there is less of preaching and of forced moral. Hector's defiance of augury is the tone of the whole Iliad. There is no hint in Homer, for instance, of the later moralisation that he was betrayed by the armour of Patroclus, or dragged in death by the belt that had been a gift from Aias. The relation of man to the divine powers is one rather of traditional respect than of either love or fear. They are but secondary aids to man's own strength of spirit and sense of right. While on the whole the Gods love righteousness and hate iniquity, while their vengeance is conceived to follow, sooner or later, any abnormal transgression, it is neither necessary nor safe to carry this doctrine into particulars; if the matter be pressed further, they are found partial, jealous, unscrupulous. The general attitude towards religion is, to put it in modern terms, undogmatic and undenominational. It may best be illustrated by an often-quoted passage of the Odyssey. Peisistratus in Pylos lays the cup in the hands of the stranger, bidding him make libation from it and pass it on to his companion: "He, too," he adds, "no doubt prays to those who die not, for all mankind require Gods." The stranger, who is Athena in person, not only accepts this statement as adequate, but is highly pleased by its good sense.[1] More exact identification of Athena may be left to the theologians.

The famous simile of the devastating autumn floods in the Iliad approaches the Hesiodic spirit:[2] they are sent by Zeus in anger against those "who judge crooked judgments in the market-place with a high hand;" but the suffering comes not on the powerful wrong-doers, but on the people: *μινύθει δέ τε ἔργ' ἀνθρώπων*—"the industries of men" (Hesiod's very phrase) "are minished." We have a touch of the Hesiodic world in other similes, such as that of the poor widow waking to earn her children's bread, or in the repeated mention of disinherited or portionless men who have taken service as mercenaries. Akin to the Hesiodic spirit, too, is the heavy humour of the Homeric captains; the clumsy jest of Patroclus over Kebriones, which pleases him so that he has to repeat it three times over; or the chaff of Idomeneus about marrying a daughter of Agamemnon.[3] "I am a great eater of beef," any one of them might say who thought about it, "and I believe that does harm to my wit." The Menelaus of the Odyssey, a character singularly like the Theseus of *A Midsummer Night's Dream*, is first cousin to Hesiod's oppressors, the close-fisted, heavy-handed Boeotian country gentlemen. His fancy of expropriating the population of a whole village to provide an estate for a friend, his suggestion to that friend's son of a tour through the country with the view of picking up some portable property in each

[1] *Od.* iii. 40–52.

[2] *Il.* xvi. 384–92.

[3] *Il.* xvi. 745–50, xiii. 378.

town they visited,[1] would have invited very Hesiodic comments from the people immediately concerned.

But nothing in Homer hints at what is felt as an undertone in Hesiod, the coming of democracy, the self-consciousness of a whole people. Not long, as length of time is measured in the history of human development, after the Iliad took its final shape, the world swung into a new course. Hellas crowned and killed the epic. Only after Hellas had come to be absorbed in a half-Hellenised world did men of letters begin, like the architects of revived Gothic in the nineteenth century, to build anew in imitation of the mediaeval manner. In neither attempt was there any enduring life.

Before this great change had happened, or while it was happening, came the final construction of the Odyssey. It is a significant fact that criticism of Homer, where the Odyssey is not specifically in question, has always tended to become criticism of the Iliad. Whatever difference of opinion there may be as to the relative merit or the relative charm of the two poems, no one could deny that the earlier is also the greater. If we are to give a reason why this is so, it seems to be that the epic realised its full potencies in the Iliad—ἔσχε φύσιν—just at the brief culminating time of the formative imagination while it worked in the epic material. Our Odyssey is held by scholars from considerations of language to be at least a generation later than our Iliad. Considering it as poetry we arrive at exactly the

[1] *Od.* iv. 174–7, xv. 79–85.

same conclusion. It implies the Iliad, as the architecture of the fourteenth century implies that of the thirteenth. It attempts a further advance upon an altered method. But in it poetry burns at a lower heat. A similar change passed over mediaeval architecture with great rapidity towards the end of the thirteenth century. Men tried to repeat and outdo what had been done to perfection by their predecessors. They produced work more ingenious, more daring in construction, more richly ornamented. But it had the seeds of weakness in it; we begin to foresee the end. The imagination of the artist who produced the Iliad is felt at a furnace-heat through the whole poem, even where he left great pieces of earlier work practically untouched, where they did not wholly fuse and coalesce. The Odyssey is planned more ambitiously, more dexterously; construction is passing from an art into a science, architecture into engineering. Nothing in the Iliad is such a feat of design as the way in which the first four books of the Odyssey do not bring Odysseus on to the scene at all and yet imply him through every line as the central figure. A faultless sense of proportion keeps the poem wholly clear of divided interest. But, from whatever reasons, the genius flagged later. The Odyssey reminds one of a church begun when architecture had reached its perfection, on which the age lavished all its skill and riches, but where the imaginative impulse gave out before it was completed, or where part of the structure, built hastily or recklessly, collapsed and was rebuilt poorly by feebler hands. It stands to the Iliad in somewhat the same relation as the Cathedral of Beauvais does to that of Chartres. These two churches are not more than twenty or thirty years apart; and it is not certain that a longer interval separates the two poems. But we have no contemporary records, no authentic tradition, to help us to decide.

All through, even where it is at its best, even in the matchless sixth and thirteenth books, we have this sense that the Odyssey is at a lower heat than the Iliad. Up to Book XIX. nothing can be more admirable than its construction. But it is built up, not run into the mould while still incandescent. The difference in the opening of the two poems is characteristic. Instead of the great triple-bayed porch, high-vaulted and glowing with colour, through which we approach the main action of the Odyssey in the three successive acts that unroll themselves at Ithaca, at Pylos, at Lacedaemon, we pass through a simple door and at one step are in the vast nave of the Iliad. The subject is set out with extreme though masterly rapidity. In the first two hundred and fifty lines we have Achilles and Agamemnon, Aias, Idomeneus, Calchas, Odysseus, Nestor, Priam and man-slaying Hector, Clytemnestra, Briseis. None of them are explained; the artist is perfectly sure of himself and of them. Through all the Iliad there is this fiery rapidity. Yet it is combined with extraordinary leisureliness. This has to be borne in mind when we speak of two notes of Homer being that he is uniformly plain and uniformly rapid. No poet can be more terse or more diffuse, more simple or more elaborate. Two scenes in the Iliad may be cited as showing these qualities in vivid contrast. One is the episode of Glaucus and Diomede in Book VI. Their meeting is told in two lines; then over a hundred are filled by their splendid and richly embroidered speeches. These include the stories of the frenzy of Lycurgus and the life and death of Bellerophon, the latter introduced by that noble simile of the forest leaves which includes the best-known single line in Homer. The other is the last battle of Hector in Book XXII. The anguish of that hour is drawn out almost beyond endurance; it seems to be going on almost for ever, as in a dream. The action stands still, advances, recedes. An endless dreary procession of thought circles through Hector's mind while retreat is still possible, like the vision of a whole lifetime rising before a drowning man: the reproach of Polydamas; the sickening thought of being put to shame before the Trojan women; the awful sense of his own fatal error of judgment, for which only death can atone; idle thoughts of giving up everything for which the war was fought, and the recognition of their uselessness; at last, in all but intolerable poignancy, that strange vision of his own youth, and a boy and girl whispering soft words to each other. Then comes the dreadful moment when his courage breaks down; the long hopeless flight and fierce pursuit; the gleam of hope and recovery of self-control; the desperate rush at Achilles when the goddess has tricked him out of his spear. Again and again we seem at the very climax, and again and again it is deferred. At last it comes. The spear-head crashes through his neck, and all is over but the last gasping words of the dying man and Achilles' reply, swift now, terse, edged like bronze.

"Well I know thee and see thee as thou art, nor was I to persuade thee; for verily thy heart is iron within thee. Look to it now lest I become a Wrath of the Gods on thee in the day when Paris and Phoebus Apollo shall slay thee, for all thy valour, in the Scaean gates."

"Lie dead: and I will accept my weird whensoever Zeus and the deathless Gods are pleased to accomplish it."

It is this combination of fiery speed and all but stationary movement that makes the Iliad unique. The movement of the Odyssey is more equable and slower. The artifice of rhythmic construction is used with perfect ease and mastery, and lends itself to a treatment less elastic but more flexible. I can here merely indicate the way in which it is applied to two main motives in the Odyssey. One of these is the story of Odysseus' own adventures between the fall of Troy and the opening of the action. The other is the story of the fatal home-coming of Agamemnon, against which the triumphant return of Odysseus is throughout set in sharp relief. Both are given briefly by Zeus in Book I. The latter is repeated first by Athena to Telemachus, again by Nestor at Pylos, again by Menelaus at Sparta as it had been told him by the sea-wizard, yet again by the ghost of Agamemnon himself in the Summoning of the Dead. But the variations are so skilful and so apt that there is no sense of mere repetition, only of cumulative effect. So likewise with the tales of his own adventures told by Odysseus. Of these there are no less than seven: the stories told to Nausicaa in Book VI., to Arete and Alcinous in Book VII., to the whole Phaeacian court in Books IX. to XII.; the adroit, swiftly-invented account he gives of himself to Athena when he meets her on the beach in the heavy morning mist; the elaborate and plausible romance told to Eumaeus in Book XIV., and partly repeated to Antinous, with such modifications as suited the immediate occasion, in Book XVII.; finally, the extraordinary story he tells to Penelope on the very eve of the suitor-slaying, for no other reason, as it would seem, beyond sheer excitement and delight in his own powers of invention. In these and other instances the devices of postponement and varied repetition are used with perfect skill and effect up to the crisis of the action, the scene in the hall at Ithaca towards which the whole poem has been leading, when all the company gradually go out, Athena holds the cresset while Telemachus and his father remove the armour, and at last, by the glimmer of the midnight fire, Odysseus and Penelope are face to face alone.

And then nothing happens. Just at this point the constructive power, until then masterly and faultless, gives way; and the end of the Odyssey, to put it bluntly, is bungled. The artifice of postponement has been tried once too often; and though all the resources of poetry are lavished on it, the action is only set agoing again by an obvious effort. There are still indeed incidents and passages of great beauty. Nothing could be finer than the vision of Theoclymenus at the banquet, when he cries out that the sun is eclipsed, and sees the suitors wrapped in a pall of night, with tears running down their cheeks, and blood spattered on the walls; or the scene of the actual drawing of the bow; or that where Odysseus strips off his beggar's rags and leaps up tense and erect on the door-sill, pouring the arrows down before his feet; or the summoning of Eurycleia from the locked house where nothing had been seen and nothing heard except scuffling and groans, to find Odysseus standing in the hall alone, and round him a great pile of dead men. But the trial of the bow is introduced clumsily, with insufficient motive; details of the battle in the hall have been noted by all critics as partly inconsistent and partly unintelligible. The action is merely retarded by the arrival of Philoetius by the ferry, and the fresh insults of Ctesippus; here, and still more so in the scene known as the Second Summoning of the Dead, the artifice of repetition, like the artifice of postponement, is used once too often, and with inferior skill; and then the poem is huddled up to a scrappy, strained, ineffective conclusion. The best Alexandrian critics saw in the whole of the twenty-fourth and a portion of the twenty-third book the work of a continuator. This may be so; but it is earlier that the organic structure and movement begin to break down. The exact turning point is the speech of Penelope in lines 509 to 553 of Book XIX. It is a brilliant and desperate effort to regain the high tension that had been let slack in the *Niptra.* It includes the famous nightingale-simile, a perfect miracle of language, but language that is passing from epic into lyric. Penelope's description of her dream and awakening which follows it, is nearly as remarkable; it has a simplicity almost like that of Wordsworth; but we feel in it just a suspicion of *simplesse;* its tone is that not of the epic but of the idyl. With all its mixed lyric and idyllic beauty, the passage is in its artifice less Homeric than Tennysonian. It is the swan-note of the dying epic. We have passed at one step, as it were, from Homer to Theocritus.

Once this step had been taken, it could not be retraced. The change is not in language, nor in metre, nor superficially at least, in handling; it is a change in the meaning of poetry. And this in turn is due to a change in the way of regarding and interpreting life. Now and then in Homer, but very rarely, we come on a passage like that of the pigeon-shooting in Book XXIII. of the Iliad, which we can say at the first glance and without hesitation is un-Homeric, which stands as glaringly apart from its surroundings as a seventeenth-century monument in a thirteenth-century church. But the difference in spirit is generally much subtler and more indefinable. For testing what is really Homeric, this changed spirit, and not apparent imitation or repetition, is the touchstone to be applied.

All art is imitation; all mediaeval art is founded on repetition. The artifice of repetition, clearly present as a structural principle in the Iliad, and used with such elaborate skill in the design of the Odyssey, is characteristic of both the Iliad and Odyssey in its application to language. Much certainly, probably most, of what is suspected as copying by a later hand is deliberate and original; like the recurrence, with subtle variations, of the patterned figures in a tapestry or the carved figures in a processional frieze. For the genius of the epic this kind of repetition was an essential element in design. We judge all these kinds of art stupidly, if we apply to them rules of composition and perspective which are relevant to other and later kinds of art. Whether on a larger or on a smaller scale this has always to be borne in mind with Homer. We misjudge the *Aristeia* of the captains—Aias, or Diomede, or Idomeneus—in their relation to the scheme of the Iliad, if we fail to realise that the epic perspective, like that of the early painting, represents the secondary planes on practically the same scale as the primary. Let me quote some luminous words of Burne-Jones, given in his Life, regarding the theory and practice of mediaeval art as it was understood by the two artists who in our own times were most in sympathy with it. "We have lost one thing in the world," he says, "which we need never expect to get back again, and that is the right to put a figure n the background of the same size as those in the front. The Greeks did it, and the old Italians, and it used to be quite right, but we can't any longer.

Figures diminished by distance are a bore. Morris, who was so rightly minded, as he always was, had a very true saying about it. He was fond of insisting that heads in decoration ought to be of exactly the same size, and go one just behind the other like shillings in a row." The art of Homer, it cannot be too much kept in mind, is in many essentials, like his world, mediaeval.

Just so likewise we misjudge the repetition of lines or phrases or passages, if we forget that such repetition was, like that of flowers in a tapestry or diapers in a painting, deliberate in the artist and delightful to his audience. It is in view of this that we must regard what has been called epic slang, the lavish, repeated use of stock epithets, stock phrases, stock incidents or reflections—all that a more fastidious taste or a more easily exhausted interest disparages as the journalism of the epic.

In the process through which poetry comes into existence at all, this note of repetition, of pattern, is an essential element. Some patterns are mechanical; but that is a very different thing from saying that art can dispense with pattern. It is difficult to say—and certainly the artist could not say himself—at what point the evolution of pattern ceases to be creative and becomes a mechanism, or a trick. The question has been raised, and keenly debated, in other forms of art than poetry—one notable instance is as regards Mozart's music. The inspiration—to use that convenient word without being committed to any of its various meanings—fluctuates between limits which are not clearly assignable. It will be a matter partly of artistic sensitiveness, partly of trained judgment, partly of sympathy between the poet and the reader of the poetry, to distinguish in Homer or in any other poet, the illuminating from the otiose epithet, the imaginative or musical wording of a phrase from the formulary tag, the impassioned statement of truth from the truism or commonplace. The fire of poetry burns at varying degrees in any large poem; its living and quickening power were not originally the same throughout, and have withstood the action of time still more variably. The business of its interpreters, the reward of its lovers, is to revitalise as much of it as possible. This is a work implying thought and study as well as sympathy. No labour is wasted in this thought and study; for we shall often find after it, that the dull line or phrase or passage becomes irradiated; that we see at last what we are meant to see, and feel as the poet felt. It is in such a way that the interpretation of poetry, the otherwise arid task of the commentator, may be of real use.

Perhaps of all the ornaments of style the epithet is the one which has been, and is, most abused in poetry, or for that matter in prose. "Very good orators, when they are out," Rosalind tells us, "they will spit;" and for poets lacking matter the cleanliest shift is to fall back on epithets, which like rouge and padding are meant to conceal—while they often in fact emphasise—the want of real colour and substance. But in its inception, and in its proper use, the epithet has the effect of immensely increasing and enriching the poet's vocabulary. Not attached to the word as an ornament, but welded on to it as an integral part of the meaning, it yields an unlimited supply of what are in effect new words, free from the harshness of novelty, easily understood, adaptable to the expression of varying shades of meaning. By the variation of epithets the poet has command of a whole set of verbal symbols to express a single thing or person in different aspects, at different angles, in the reflected colour of different surroundings. Poetry, when the Iliad and Odyssey took shape, had become a matured art with its recognised symbols, counters that had already worn smooth or were wearing smooth by use. But these symbols in most cases must have still retained much of their original value; they were not interchangeable; each stood for something definite to the poet's imagination, and conveyed a substantive meaning to his hearers. To realise that meaning often enables us to recapture a whole point of view, even a whole aspect of life or nature as it presented itself to the poet, that we should otherwise have missed.

Various kinds of epithet may be distinguished in Homer. There is the proper or established attribute, which is so associated with its subject that it may be used almost indifferently with or without the noun substantive. This often carries something of a ritual or hieratic significance. The Cloud-Gathering, the Grey-Eyed, the Golden-Spindled are epithets well on their way to becoming proper names, like the Virgin or the Almighty. So, too, with princes and heroes;

the Fleet-Footed and the Many-Counselled are known without any further name as the principal figures of the Iliad and Odyssey: so even with natural objects invested with some special sacredness; we find the Wet spoken of simply, alongside of the fuller phrase that speaks of the wet paths of the sea.

Again, there is a whole class which name a place or object in what we might call its heraldic colours; thus it is that Homer speaks of windy Troy, wide-lawned Elis, hollow-sunken Lacedaemon, horse-pasturing Argos. Or we have a whole group of words that are attached on different occasions to the same object, and reflect light on one another. Such are the epithets "rose-footed" and "saffron-gowned" applied to dawn; such, applied to the sea, is a group of three, "violet-coloured," "wine-bright," "unvintaged." They are used singly, never together; but each implies the others, and they convey (or any one of them conveys in the reflected light of the others) a complex image, not descriptive only but in the highest degree imaginative. Other complex epithets are so curiously constructed as to make a whole picture by themselves, without interrupting the movement of the poem by a long parenthesis, or burdening it with a formal description. These are peculiarly Homeric in the richness of their sound as well as of their meaning; words like ἁλιμυρήεντα, εἰνοσίφυλλον, αἰθρηγενέτης, the "seaward-murmuring river," the "foliage-tossing mountain," the "crystal-cradled north wind." Two of them applied to war, "man-ennobling" and "mortal-destroying"—βροτολοιγός and κυδιάνειρα—give between them something of the whole moral purpose of the Iliad.

We cannot always read such meaning into the Homeric epithets. Sometimes they seem to be used from mere habit; sometimes more to fill up a line than for any larger purpose; sometimes for simple pleasure, from intoxication with the beauty of sound which even now is irresistible in Homer, and which must have meant so much more when it was all new. As the raw material of poetry, the Greek language stands alone. A language that can, quite simply and unaffectedly, render the words "from ships and huts" by *νεῶν ἄπο καὶ κλισιάων*, or "sunrise" by *ἀντολαὶ ἠελίοιο*, has no need to bolster itself out with merely ornamental epithets; yet to this beauty of sound the epithets contribute largely, and often we need look no farther than this for their motive, or at least for their justification.

Consider now a poetical ornament on a larger scale, which is equally characteristic in Homer, the simile. In poetry of a low heat this tends to become merely ornamental. It serves to enrich a passage which would otherwise be bald or languid; and, as such passages will occur in a long narrative poem, it has its legitimate use for that purpose. But in poetry of a high temperature any enrichment which is mere decoration is out of place; it only interrupts and retards, unless together with its quality as ornament it illuminates its context. This it can do by throwing a fresh imaginative light on the action to which it is attached, either by reinforcing it or, which is the more frequent use, by relieving it upon a background differing in tone, yet such that the two tones produce a single harmony. In all these uses the Homeric simile reached perfection. The nightingale passage in the Odyssey, to which reference has already been made, is perhaps the best instance of a simile used for purely decorative value. But there, as we noted, it is on the edge of misuse. It is an ornament detachable without loss, and therefore for the essential purposes of the poem irrelevant in spite of its great beauty. It would be easy to instance a score of others, in both Iliad and Odyssey, which to a like beauty of language add the imaginative light, and become part of the essence of the scene or action they illustrate: that, for instance, of the rain-drooped poppy, in "some tempestuous morn in early June," καρπῷ βριθομένη νοτίῃσί τε εἰαρινῇσιν, to which the son of Priam is compared as he sinks under the arrow of Teucer; or that of the sea churned into crested blackness by cross winds and covering the beach with seaweed, used as a comparison for the confusion and gloom of the Achaean army when they have been driven back on the ships and only nightfall has saved them from utter rout; or that of the great snowfall, "on a winter day when Zeus the Counsellor has set him to snow, and lulls the winds and snows continually, until he has covered the high hill-peaks and jutting headlands, and the grassy plains and rich tillage of men," to which is compared the thick shower of stones from both sides in the fast-locked battle at the wall.[1] In other instances enrichment is accumulated

[1] *Il.* viii. 306–8, ix. 4–7, xii. 278–286.

in order to dilute rather than to concentrate; not to add imaginative value to the action, but because the action is at so high a tension that it requires relief, that it not only will bear any amount of decoration, but demands it. Such is the triple inverted simile which introduces the rally of the Achaeans when pent in on the beach, where the sea washed up to the Argive huts and ships; and the shouting of the charging hosts was so terrible that neither thunder of breakers, nor the roar of blazing fire, nor the voice of the furious wind was like to it.[1] Or enriched ornament may be used, not where the action is at a higher tension, but where it is more formal and stately. The celebrated instance is the accumulation of no less than six fully elaborated similes before the Catalogue in Book II. of the Iliad, like trumpets sounding over a clear space before the coming of a great procession. Most commonly, however, these comparisons reflect upon some tense situation or violent action the quietness of nature or of natural things; often with a sense of beauty more delicate and observant than we find again until nature was looked on by the eyes of Western Europe, and with a feeling for the beauty of common life which keeps the atmosphere of the poem cool and sane. Such are the pictures of the hawk poising above the cliff; of the slim-foliaged ash seen against the sky on a hill; of the blossomed olive grown in a solitary place where a spring bubbles up, and it is blown by all the breezes and shimmers into silver; of the woodman preparing his dinner in a dell

[1] *Il.* xiv. 392–401.

among the hills, or the gardener guiding runlets of water from a spring to ripple down over the trenched slopes of his garden-plot.[1] The invention of this class of ornament has been staled by use; and it lends itself with horrid facility to the hands of the minor poet. But it was an invention of the first importance; and it has never been used with greater tact and skill than in the Homeric poetry where it makes its first appearance. The effect of these spaces of cool air and quiet daylight in the composition is magical. One more instance may be quoted, not only for its own beauty of language but for the way in which it interlaces the themes of the Iliad and Odyssey. On the voyage from Aeolia, just before Odysseus succumbs to sleep, outworn by superhuman watchings, "On the tenth day," he says, "the tilled fields of my native land came in sight, and now we were so near that we saw the kindling of fires." The same situation is used in the Iliad as a piece of rich ornament in the description of the going forth of Achilles to battle. "As when over the sea there appears to sailors the brightness of a burning fire, that burns high among the hills in a lonely farm; then storm-blasts bear them off unwilling over the sea, where the fishes go, far from their own people." The picture is the same, but the point of view is reversed.[2] Not otherwise might a Tuscan or Umbrian painter of the fifteenth century, Piero di Cosimo or Pinturicchio, show, through a window in his picture, a background of sea with the

[1] *Il.* xiii. 60, 180, xvii. 53–6, xi. 86–9, xxi. 257–62.

[2] *Il.* xix. 375–8; *Od.* x. 29, 30.

ship of Odysseus and the points of fire on the dusking island.

But it is neither by his epithets nor by his similes, nor by that kind of ornament which these two specific means of poetical effect represent, that a poet takes his rank, or that great poetry is created. For that we have to turn to a higher plane of thought and feeling. The saying that poetry is a criticism of life has this much of truth in it, that poetry depends on its grasp of life for high poetic quality. It is here that all generations have instinctively felt the greatness of the Homeric poems. Their whole view and handling of life, not as a mere pageant but as the arena of great energies, are unsurpassed in elevation and completeness. In them human life is poised among vast spiritual forces, and glitters "like a jewel hung in ghastly night" against a dark background lit up by splendid courage, clear insight, unconquerable will. The spirit of man rises in them beyond circumstance, beyond divine control, even beyond fate. Only in the Northern Sagas (the ancestral epic of our own race as Homer was of the Greek) is man so great, and the moral effect of the poetry, as distinct from its moral lesson, from the specific truths to be drawn from it, so uplifting and so sustaining. In this sense the lines of Horace in which he sets Homer above the Greek philosophers express what is true of him as it is true of all the highest poetry. To this splendid energy of human life the Gods, "who live easily," take really a second place. When Zeus sits on the mountain summit "rejoicing in his glory, looking on Troy town and the

Achaean ships," it is they and not he who are at the centre of the interest. The picture, at the end of Book I. of the Iliad, of the day-long feast in Olympus, where the Muses sing to the viol of Apollo, is the implied background throughout to a foreground which gives the more impressive spectacle of earth, with its war and wandering, its burden of toil and trouble and death. The Homeric idealisation of life is not in any such golden world, above or below earth, in a conjectured future or a fabulous past, but in the actual deeds of men, so predestined and so accomplished that they become a song for times to be.

This unmatched power to express the sense of human greatness is what above all else makes Homer, in the phrase applied to him by a later Greek poet, "the ageless mouth of the world." It is concentrated in such words as the famous "Forward"—ἴομεν—of Sarpedon; the "Endure, O heart," of Odysseus; Hector's "One omen is best, to defend the fatherland." So, too, a whole criticism of life is concentrated in many passages that have become keywords for mankind: the words of Zeus in the prologue to the Odyssey, "Alas, how idly do mortals blame the Gods, saying that from us come their evils, while they themselves by their own infatuation have sorrows beyond what is ordained;" or the lines that occur in both Iliad and Odyssey, "Howbeit hereafter shall he suffer whatsoever fate spun for him with the thread at birth, when his mother bore him;" or the summing up of the joy of life in the words of Odysseus, "Better and fairer is nothing than this, when husband and wife keep house together with one heart and mind between them, and they themselves know it best;" or of its sorrow in those of Menelaus, "Of all things comes satiety, even of love and sleep and of sweet singing, though of these a man would sooner take his fill than of battle."[1] So it is, too, pre-eminently in two more passages: one the famous sentence of Glaucus, which has never lost its freshness or its piercing beauty through millionfold repetition: "Why enquire of my lineage? Even as the generations of leaves are those of men: the leaves that be, them the wind scatters on earth, but the woodland buds and puts forth more again when the season of spring comes on; so of the generations of men one springs up and another passes away:" the other, perhaps the most remarkable of all, the words put in the mouth of Paris, as if to show that it is not always to the greatest of her children that life gives her largest wisdom: "Not to be thrown away are the gifts of the Gods, that they give unbidden, and no man may have them of his own choice."[2]

Texts like these have become the commonplaces of thought, the stock-in-trade of secondary poets; like the epithet and the simile, the moral sentence conveying a light on the whole of life can be degraded until it fails to convey any meaning, or to be a mark for the ways of men. As with those ornaments it is our business to see them with our own eyes and feel them with our own senses, so it is our business with these to reconstitute them by our imagination as they were first

[1] *Od.* i. 32–4; *Il.* xx. 127, 8; *Od.* vii. 197, 8, vi. 182–5; *Il.* xiii. 636–9.
[2] *Il.* vi. 145–9, iii. 65, 6.

imagined. In each case let me take one concrete instance in order to illustrate and emphasise a meaning which, when stated in general terms, may itself become a mere commonplace.

"A single epithet in Homer," says Mr. Butcher in his admirable Harvard lectures, "will often open up to us the very heart of the object." I take the first instance that comes to hand. The word λευκώλενος, "white-armed," is one of the common Homeric epithets applied to women. Many thousands of readers must have slipped over it as a mere indolent ornamental epithet, a piece of prettiness at the best, if not a tag to fill up the verse. How many are there who have paused long enough over it to consider what it means? How many, even if they realised its meaning, have grasped what it implies? The women of Homer are not the white-handed ladies of a literary convention, nor the creatures of a luxurious civilisation who toil not neither spin. Had Odysseus complimented Nausicaa as white-handed after her morning's work by the river, he would probably have moved her to some expression of that fresh humour with which later she imitates the talk of her vulgar townspeople. But let us take a passage from the most Homeric of English poets and flash it upon this single Homeric word. "My hands are burned," says the heroine in *Mother and Son*,

> By the lovely sun of the acres;
>   But lo, where the edge of the gown
> (So said thy father) is parting
>   The wrist that is white as the curd
> From the brown of the hand that I love,
>   Bright as the wing of a bird.

The lines are little more than an expansion of the single Homeric epithet. It is charged with the whole aspect of a simpler and stronger life than our own. Under this fresh light the idle epithet has become a living and revealing word.

Take again one of the developed similes in the Iliad, famous indeed but strangely misinterpreted by the commentators, and curiously overshadowed in general appreciation by another. That other, in the description of the Trojan camp at night in the eighth book, is universally known; it is the instance which has been used, ever since Wordsworth's Supplementary Preface to the Poems of 1815, for the purposes of criticism on the poetical diction of the eighteenth century, as represented by Pope's translation; and the passage in which it occurs was chosen by Tennyson for an experiment in translation of his own. It may be noticed in passing that, apart from the larger question of style, Pope is to be excused if he failed to give a satisfactory rendering of a picture with which, in the original, something seems to have gone wrong. The passage to which I wish to draw attention, and of which, according to the modern critics, that in Book VIII. is an adaptation by a later poet, is in Book XVI. It is at a culminating point of the action. Patroclus, in the armour of Achilles, has come out to save the day where the battle is fiercest round the ship of Protesilaus. His first spear-cast strikes down a Paeonian captain. A thrill of horror runs through the whole Trojan ranks—ἐκίνηθεν δὲ φάλαγγες. For a minute they think that the son of Peleus himself is upon them, and remain, as it were, frozen to the ground where they stand. Then they break in rout, and the roar of battle goes up again.

That minute's awful pause is illuminated by an image which is unsurpassed both in its vivid truth and in its imaginative fitness—

> *ὡς δ' ὅτ' ἀφ' ὑψηλῆς κορυφῆς ὄρεος μεγάλοιο*
> *κινήσῃ πυκινὴν νεφέλην στεροπηγερέτα Ζεύς,*
> *ἔκ τ' ἔφανεν πᾶσαι σκοπιαὶ καὶ πρώονες ἄκροι*
> *καὶ νάπαι, οὐρανόθεν δ' ἄρ' ὑπερράγη ἄσπετος αἰθήρ.*

"As when from the great crest of a high hill Zeus the Lightning-gatherer pierces the dense cloud, and of a sudden all the peaks and jutting spurs and dells shine out, and in heaven the illimitable sky is rent asunder; such was the breathing space."[1] The picture is given in four lines. Let us again see how a modern writer, getting his effect not by one broad sweep of the brush but by minute accumulated touches, describes the same thing happening.

"It might have been a lantern that was flashed across the hill. Then all that part of the world went suddenly on fire. Everything was horribly distinct in that white light. The firs of Caddam were so near that it seemed to have arrested them in a silent march upon the hill. The grass would not hide a pebble. The ground was scored with shadows of men and things. Twice the light flickered and recovered itself. A red serpent shot across it, and then again black night fell. The hill had been illumined thus for

[1] *Il.* xvi. 297–300.

nearly half a minute. During that time not even a dog stirred."

If it would be too much to say that all this description is latent in the Homeric simile, yet in the light of it the Homeric simile is seen to mean more, to have a more exact relevance and a greater imaginative value: above all, we shall see that the brief explanatory note in the Scholia, *τουτέστιν ἀστραπὴ ἐγένετο*, is exactly correct, and shall be saved from the stupidity of regarding the description as merely that of "a gleaming crag with belts of pines" discovered through a rift in the mist.

Or once more, let us apply the same interpretative method to one of Homer's great ethical lines. I take one which is so familiar that it almost ceases to stir us unless we use real effort to re-create the imaginative impulse which produced it: the famous *αἰὲν ἀριστεύειν καὶ ὑπείροχον ἔμμεναι ἄλλων*. It occurs twice in the Iliad, in each case as the maxim of a heroic father: the words are those of Hippolochus to Glaucus, and those of Peleus to Achilles, when they sent their sons forth to the war.[1] "He sent me to Troy," says Glaucus, "and charged me full often to be ever a valiant man and to excel others." "Aged Peleus," says Nestor to Patroclus, "charged his son Achilles to be ever a valiant man and to excel others; but to you Menoetius son of Actor gave charge thus"—and so forth, four lines of excellent advice which I need not quote.

Here the best help is in Pope's translation: for Pope, whatever his shortcomings, is always responsive

[1] *Il.* vi. 208, xi. 784.

to such passages, and kindles to the heroic temper. His two renderings are curiously different—

By his decree I sought the Trojan town;
By his instructions learn *to win renown:*
To stand the first in worth as in command,
To add new honours to my native land,
Before my eyes my mighty sires to place
And emulate the glories of our race.

That is one; now hear the other—

Your ancient fathers generous precepts gave:
Peleus said only this: My son, *be brave.*

Which of these is the better translation—the four and a half lines or the two words? The question is idle: for both are perfect. In the light of either, still more in the light of both, the line of Homer becomes alive. The gorgeous amplification of the one rendering, the concentrated brevity of the other, both go straight to the mark, and give the same lifting of the heart. In them the Homeric sentence has once more become reillumined with its first brightness, recharged with its first significance.

It is a part of the power of great poetry to find a soul of goodness in things evil or indifferent, to walk through the fire unscathed and carry from it light in the darkness and comfortable heat for men. The morals of Homer's world are not high-pitched, nor are his characters uniformly admirable. He was too great an artist to make them so, or to make us wish he had. Hector shows more than once something approaching cowardice. Odysseus is perfectly unscrupulous in disregard of truth, and in both Iliad and

Odyssey his character has a sinister element of cruelty. In both Iliad and Odyssey Helen speaks of herself as a shameless worker of evil quite placidly and without the least heart-sorrow. Yet the whole effect of Homer is to exalt courage, purity, straightforwardness, mercy.

So also in both Iliad and Odyssey the sombre view of human life, though most prominently felt by Achilles and expressed by him in language of the darkest magnificence, is never far off anywhere. And yet the elasticity and radiance of life are the final and lasting impression left by Homer; he has to all later ages embodied the *iuventus mundi;* his world is one where, as in the magic island of Circe, are the dwellings and dancing-grounds of Dawn of Morning, and the uprisings of the sun.

It is through this quality, the incarnation of the whole strength and splendour of life, that Homer holds the place given him by Lucretius and Dante as sovereign of the poets. It is one for which even praise seems inadequate or inappropriate. Somehow or other we praise Homer, it has been said, too like barbarians. The mistake perhaps rather lies in our praising him at all; as Swinburne says of Shakespeare, "His praise is this, that he is praised of none." One may imagine him replying to his panegyrists as to his critics in the noble words of Odysseus to Diomede—

μήτ' ἄρ με μάλ' αἴνεε, μήτε τι νείκει·
ἀλλ' ἴομεν· μάλα γὰρ νὺξ ἄνεται, ἐγγύθι δ' ἠώς.

"Praise me not much, neither blame me, but let us go forward; for night is far spent, and the dawn is nigh."[1]

[1] *Il.* x. 249–51.

THE LYRIC POETS

I

THE AGE OF FREEDOM: SAPPHO

Τᾶμος ἄϋπνος κλυτὸς ὄρθρος ἐγείρησιν ἀηδόνας—"Then sleepless magnificent dawn awakes the nightingales:" this stray line from one of the nine lyrists of the Greek canon, preserved for us by being quoted in a treatise on grammar written in the reign of Marcus Aurelius,[1] might well be placed as a motto over the fragmentary but priceless volume of the Greek lyric poets. The splendid epic sunset is followed by a profound night of between one and two centuries. That night wore on, the voice of the epic sounding fainter and fainter across it,

> Till waned the moon and all the stars grew pale,
> And from the east faint yellow light outshone
> O'er the Greek sea, so many years agone.

In the intervening period of darkness, hardly recoverable even in the main outlines of its history, and without any authentic record of its literature, the Hellenic race had been born. Histories of Greece present us with a confused record of migrations, conquests, and colonisations, amid which the mediaeval framework of life pictured in the Homeric poems completely disappeared. With the memory of the

[1] Ibycus, frag. 7.

Homeric life, the memory even of the Homeric poetry became confused and dispersed. All the ancient world was broken up. The beginnings of the lyric, so far as they can be traced by recoverable fragments, do not take us back much beyond 700 B.C. At that time Hellenic life in many of its aspects, and Hellenic thought in some of its distinctive qualities, were already established. Monarchy had been abolished at Athens and Corinth. The constitution of Lycurgus was already of ancient date at Sparta. The Greek colonies beyond the seas had become thriving independent powers. The thalassocracy of Miletus, a movement which if developed might have placed the centre of Greek life on the eastern coasts of the Aegean and turned the whole course of human history, had not yet fallen before the pressure of the Lydian empire. The epoch of the tyrants was approaching. As in the Tudor period in England, these hereditary monarchies, while they reinstated old names and renewed old forms, were based on a completely different theory of government from that of the mediaeval Homeric world, and were the first stage in the evolution of democracy. In the birth of Greek poetry and its development during the seventh and sixth centuries B.C. may be traced three different threads, interwoven it is true with great complexity, yet to a certain extent detachable from one another, and giving a clue to the progress of poetry between the decay of the epic and the concentration of intellectual life at Athens. There is the court poet, the lineal successor of the Homeric minstrel, living now no longer at the seat of a patriarchal or feudal government amid a life wholly based on ancestral traditions, but in the palace of one or other of the new monarchs, and adapting his poetry accordingly to the modern movement. There is the poet who, himself a member of the aristocratic class which disputed the control of the state with the joint forces of monarch and people, lives in and writes for that circle. Finally there is the poet who, detached alike from the courts of kings and from the more exclusive culture of an aristocratic class, writes for himself, and thus for the whole world. The achievement of Hellas in these ages was to create the state on one hand, to create the individual on the other. In the sphere of poetry, by an analogous double achievement, the Hellenic genius created personal and national poetry. Both took shape in the forms which are widely classed under the general name of lyrical. As including the iambic and elegiac as well as the melic poets, that name covers what is really the whole field of Greek poetry other than epic and dramatic—the epic, which is the specific product of mediaeval or pre-Hellenic Greece, and the dramatic, which is the specific product of the fully organised city-state, of the city absorbing individual life, and of poetry concentrated to a civic function.

So wide a field has no obvious or definable unity. As a matter of fact the term lyric poetry was unknown to the Greeks; and its subdivisions, iambic, elegiac, and melic, are based on an arbitrary test of metrical form in the first two, and on a connection almost as arbitrary between poetry and music in the third. With the progress and differentiation of literary forms, iambic poetry became in the main absorbed into the drama: elegiac poetry more and more tended, until it took a fresh development among the Alexandrians, towards the specific province of the epigram. The history of both these forms is very varied and fluctuating. But in what is known as the lyric age, it is on melic poetry—what may be called the lyric proper—that we may best concentrate our attention. To avoid the unfamiliar term of melic, I shall use the word lyric and lyrist henceforward in this restricted sense.

According to the metricians, Greek lyric poetry in this acceptation of the term has two notes distinctive of it in its technical or formal quality. It is in the first place strophic—a *ποίημα κατὰ περίοδον* in the phrase of the grammarians—that is to say, it is written in stanzas, and not in continuous lines of the same metrical structure. These stanzas are commonly in their simpler forms, as they are likewise in English, of four lines each; but, also as in English, they vary beyond this inferior limit up to almost any degree of length and intricacy. In the second place it is normally, though to this rule there are exceptions, "logaoedic"—that is to say, it is written not in continuous feet of the same metrical length, but in some combination of dactylic and trochaic rhythms, in a combination, that is, of common and triple time. Both of these may seem highly technical differentiae, having little to do with the quality of poetry as such. Yet they are not without importance as effects, and in turn as contributory causes, of the wholly new scope and expansion which Greek poetry took in the lyric age. They mean that in form as in spirit the established mediaeval practice has been supplemented, and even for a time superseded, by fresh movements of poetry embodying new ideals in new methods.

The earliest departure, according to such slight records as are attainable, from the dominant hexameter verse of the epic age was that modification of it which became established in the form of the elegiac couplet. This form of poetry arose in the old home of the epic, and remained in close contact with the epic traditions in language and structure. The name of rhapsodist, it has been noted, is still applied to the poets who practised it. It was a subsidiary growth of the old art of the epic minstrel. About the same time, or a little later, came the invention of the iambic, that "restless rhythm" as a historian of Greek literature well describes it, in which "the battle of life and the turmoil of the market-place found a voice"—*tönte der Streit des Lebens und der Lärm des Marktes.* If the iambicist Archilochus be held, according to the settled tradition of antiquity, as in some sense the founder of lyric poetry, this shows or at least suggests how hard was the crust of epic tradition that had to be broken. Nothing short of the voluble undignified iambic metre would do it. Once the fetters of the old tradition were broken, the lyric rapidly found its proper forms; it created for itself a versification more melodious, more delicate, more intricate and subtle in its harmonies. It was not until long after that the iambic was trained into a new scope and dignity in the hands of the Attic tragedians; and even in them it retains certain marked affinities with prose.

Both iambic and elegiac poetry had their origin in Ionia; both seem to have arisen there under some foreign and Asiatic influence, and both became fully developed somewhat later, when transplanted to the soil of Greece Proper. The traditional migration of Tyrtaeus, the first or all but the first elegist, to Sparta from Miletus, and of Archilochus, the first iambicist, to the Peloponnesus from Paros or Thasos, may be taken as a symbol of a general movement of the new forms of poetry towards the centre of Hellenic life. From that centre they spread backward again all over outer Hellas. What took place was the passage of a great wave of poetical influence from Asia to Europe and the creation under that influence of Greek poetry: that Greek poetry in turn expanding outwards to overspread the Greek world.

A similar movement took place, with equally fertile results, in lyric poetry proper. Alexandrian scholars formed, and Roman critics accepted from them, a list of nine great lyric masters. Their work, from the earliest poems of Alcman to the latest of Bacchylides, extends over a period of almost exactly two centuries. Its beginnings are in the era of the earlier Greek tyrannies like those of the Cypselids and Orthagorids, of the Lydian empire of the Mermnadae, and of the full tide of Greek colonisation over all the Mediterranean between Cyprus and Sicily. It comes to an end in the central period of fully developed Greek life between the Median and Peloponnesian wars. These centuries were a period of brilliant and restless life within the wide bounds of that whirling nebula of commonwealths which, kept apart politically by forces of mutual repulsion too powerful to be overcome, were united by a common genius into a single intellectual world. Of the nine poets, Pindar alone belonged by birth to Greece Proper. But nearly all of them, whatever the city of their origin, travelled widely beyond it in person and more widely still through their writings. Alcman of Sardis, the earliest of them in date, passed over into the Peloponnesus, and developed a highly refined, sensitive, and delicately personal poetry at Sparta: at Sparta, which of all places in the world was then the centre of the finest Hellenic culture. Sappho of Mitylene spent a considerable portion of her life in Sicily, and the legend of her death connects her with Acarnania, on the extreme verge of Hellenism. The court of Polycrates at Samos drew towards it poets not merely from the neighbouring cities, but from the distant West like Ibycus of Rhegium. As brilliant a circle were attracted to Athens and the life of intellect and scholarship which flourished there under the rule of Peisistratus. The great lyric poets of the later sixth century, Anacreon, Simonides, Pindar, Bacchylides, are recorded as travelling all over the Greek world. Towards the end of the lyric period there is a gradual concentration towards Athens; and it was here that, after the Persian wars, the new poetic art of the drama absorbed or merged into itself the double currents of iambic and lyric poetry.

The chance of history has preserved for us only inconsiderable fragments of the work of seven out of the nine great lyrists. The other two, Pindar and Bacchylides, belong to the end of the lyric age. The fiery genius of the one, the equable grace of the other, are exercised on forms and subjects which are well established, and have even begun to stiffen, and to show the first signs that the life of poetry is preparing to pass elsewhere. Lyric poetry proper after this became more and more confined to the dithyramb, a form which lent itself with fatal facility to a conventional and quasi-scientific treatment, and from which the inner spirit of poetry had passed away long before its decadence was formally recognised and registered in the work of the great innovator, Timotheus of Miletus. It is among the earlier generation of lyrists that the Greek lyric is in its first perfection, in the full charm and freshness of its youth: *χρυσοπέδιλλος αὔως*, "the gold-shod morning," *ἔαρ ὕμνων*, "the spring-tide of song."[1]

In this group of earlier lyrists the school of Lesbos takes the first place. It includes among the earlier lyrists Terpander, who like Alcman passed to Sparta and became there one of the masters in the grave and delicate Dorian lyric; among the later, Arion, the inventor or organiser of the dithyramb, not in his native country but at Corinth; between them it finds

[1] Sappho, frag. 18: Anon. in *Anth. Pal.* vii. 12, probably quoting from Erinna.

its specific native expression in the two great central names of Alcaeus and Sappho. In Alcman, a generation earlier, the flexible Ionian temperament, touched with the refined and even then somewhat severe spirit of Sparta, had wrought out a lyric poetry which we may judge from its fragments to have been of unexcelled beauty. In Tisias of Himera—the first of a family or confraternity of poets who bore the literary surname of Stesichorus, "the chorus-setter"—a mixed Doric and Chalcidian stock produced forms and methods of lyric composition which give him a place of the first importance in the historical development of Greek poetry. On one side he is still in immediate contact with the epic tradition, and came of a family which claimed some sort of descent from Hesiod: on the other hand he was, as the inventor of the fully articulated choric ode, one of the formative influences in the development of the drama; and he was also the originator of the pastoral, that specifically Sicilian type of poetry which, three hundred years later, developed as the last and one of the loveliest products of Greek genius. Between these two schools or types, Alcman and Terpander on the one hand, Stesichorus and Arion on the other, the Lesbian poets stand somewhat more apart from the general stream of poetical tendency and from mixed influences of race and surroundings. They have no certain poetical parentage, and little or no clearly visible effect on the later development of their art.

Πέρροχος ὡς ὅτ' ἄοιδος ὁ Λέσβιος ἀλλοδάποισιν—"pre-eminent, as the Lesbian singer above those of other lands"; that superb line of Sappho's[1] makes a claim for these lyrists which our best critical judgment, without a dissentient voice, willingly concedes to Sappho herself. The sole woman of any age or country who gained and still holds an unchallenged place in the first rank of the world's poets, she is also one of the few poets of whom it may be said with confidence that they hold of none and borrow of none, and that their poetry is, in some unique way, an immediate inspiration. Alcaeus, as Horace observes,[2] attracts a wider and more mixed audience. Even in Lesbos the world of men was wider and more various than the world that lay open to women. It had its thousandfold interests of war, travel, adventure, politics, society—even eating and drinking, for of these last "life consists," and they occupy a large place in Greek lyric poetry. But of the two, Sappho is the finer and more wonderful poet. The "Dorique delicacy" of Alcman, like that of a young Milton; the romantic note of Stesichorus, who reminds one again and again of a Greek Keats; the tense thrill and burning splendour of Pindar when he is most himself and most beyond comparison; the grave tenderness and high simplicity of Simonides: all these are among things priceless; but beyond them all, and when all allowance has been made for the atmosphere of legend and sentiment which has formed itself round her, Sappho seems to be, without effort and without hesitation, at the central heart of poetry. Placed beside her work that of the others seems to lose its lustre. Where simpler,

[1] Frag. 92. [2] *Odes*, II. xiii. 25–32.

it becomes thin; where more elaborate, it becomes heavy. *Sume purpuram, qualis apud nos est,* one may imagine her saying to the other poets, in the words of the Persian king to the Emperor Aurelian; and as with the gift of Bahram, so with the poetry of Sappho the historian might go on to say: *ad quod cum iungerent purpuras suas, cineris specie decolorari videbantur ceterae divini comparatione fulgoris.* Such is the feeling expressed in splendid but hardly exaggerated language by Swinburne, in that early poem where, alone among the moderns, he has mastered and all but reproduced one of her favourite metres, the Sapphic stanza which she invented and to which she gave her name—

Ah the singing, ah the delight, the passion!
All the Loves wept, listening; sick with anguish
Stood the crowned nine Muses about Apollo;
    Fear was upon them

While the tenth sang wonderful things they knew not.
Ah, the tenth, the Lesbian! the nine were silent,
None endured the sound of her song for weeping;
    Laurel by laurel

Faded all their crowns; but about her forehead
Shone a light of fire as a crown for ever.

Round the life of Sappho, and the nine books of her lyrics of which so lamentably little survives, a whole mythology, not of the most attractive nature, grew up in later Greece. It is not necessary to go into this; it would be hardly necessary to mention it, except that a word of warning is not even now superfluous against treating it seriously. In later Greece, and especially at Athens with its irreverent intellect, its dislike of romance, and its strong views with regard to the proper sphere of woman, her name became a target for audacious and often indecent witticisms. Her relations with the other lyric poets, or with the persons, whether men or women, named in her poems, supplied a field in which the Middle Comedy loved to expatiate. Later scholars, in whom all sense of humour was lost, went to these wild farces as sources of actual information. Thus Athenaeus cites a comedy of Diphilus, one of six or eight in which Sappho had the title-rôle, where Archilochus and Hipponax are introduced as two of Sappho's lovers. "I rather fancy he was joking"—*ἡγοῦμαι παίζειν*—is his perplexed comment. As Archilochus lived a century before her and Hipponax half a century after her, this conclusion does not appear to err on the side of rashness. To this puzzle-headedness was added the prurience which spread like a plague through so much of later Greek letters, and which Latin writers, for whom the Greek of the decadence was the literature that lay next them and separated them from the Greek classics, practised as a deliberate artifice. To an age of narrow prejudices, as to an age of vicious morals, a personality like that of Sappho was unintelligible. The early Ionian civilisation—one may use this term widely to cover the cities of Aeolic origin and speech as well as those of Ionia proper—seemed to them something exotic and corrupt. Lesbian vice became a proverb; and between malice and ignorance, the name of Sappho got that ugly smear across it for which her extant poetry gives no warrant, to which indeed the whole body of her extant poetry is the contradiction. In dealing with love in its aspect as a bodily passion, a poetess, even if she be Sappho, starts at some disadvantage. She has to overcome not only the conventional reticence expected of her sex, but the associations of language which have grown up in the poetry produced by men. There is a tendency for her language to swerve into the customary forms: there is a very marked tendency to more or less unconscious impersonation. Hence come ambiguities of expression which malice or prurience can distort.

Enough of this subject. But in passing from it we may just take notice of the famous Latin poem, the *Sappho Phaoni* included in some of the MSS. of Ovid's *Heroides.* That poem has done more than any other writing to give currency to the gossip of which I have spoken; at the same time it contains what are clearly renderings, and masterly renderings, of lost passages from Sappho's own poetry. The authorship of the poem has been very much disputed. While it very possibly contains interpolations by some other hand, the evidence of style is to my mind conclusive that the greater part of it is Ovid's authentic work, and that he has woven into it, with a skill and lightness of touch all his own, lines from Sappho in which we can almost feel the original. Instances of these are the *Quem supra ramos extendit aquatica lotus;* or the lovely phrasing and rhythm of the *Somnia formoso candidiora die;* or once more, the *Concinit Ismarium Daulias ales Ityn, ales Ityn,* with that reduplication of phrase which was a distinctive note in Sappho's style. These lines, while unmistakeably Ovidian, have something in them that is not Ovid; and that something is an echo of Sappho.

Of the actual Sappho what we know amounts to little or nothing. That she belonged by birth to the Lesbian aristocracy, and was born at Mitylene or Eresus about the middle of the seventh century B.C.; that she was the centre of a society of highly cultivated women who practised the arts of music and poetry in the island; that she was married and had one or more children; that in the course of some political revolution she was driven into exile with her kinsfolk and spent some years in Sicily, but returned later and died at home: these facts may be taken as fairly certain. The adventures of her brother Charaxus in Egypt do not belong to her own life. Any other details either are purely mythical or are arbitrary inferences from fragments of her poetry assumed without any reason to be autobiographic. Even the name of Sappho, "lapis-lazuli," though like Electra, "amber," or such more modern names as Margaret or Esmeralda, it may have been one of the many fanciful names given to girls in actual usage, is not improbably a self-assumed literary title, such as were habitual among Arab and Persian poets, and the tradition of which in Provence and nearer at hand in Wales continues into our own day.

In Sappho, as in the whole school of poets to which she belonged, the epic conception of poetry has completely disappeared. The hexameter is still used as one among other forms of verse; but except for this, the Homeric poems might never have existed. They were in that strange eclipse from which they reappeared a generation or two later. Among the fragments of Alcman are some which in substance approach so closely to passages in the Iliad and Odyssey that they might almost seem to be a deliberate challenge to the old by the new poetry. Such, for instance, is the passage beginning *εὕδουσιν δ' ὀρέων κορυφαί*—"The crests and clefts of the hills are asleep, and the headlands and ravines, and foliage and all moving things that the dark earth nourishes, wild hill-haunting beasts and the race of bees and the creatures in the depths of the dark-gleaming ocean, and asleep are the tribes of long-winged birds."[1] The material is that of a richly elaborated epic simile; the tone and accent, sharp, direct, personal, are those of a poetry that is finding itself afresh. Poetry has ceased to be "rhapsodia," the song-stringing and embroidery of the tale-teller. It has become the "odê" itself, the immediate utterance of personal emotion under the impact of whatever force at the moment is acting most directly on the poet.

Hence it is that the new poetry reached its full height in a civilisation like that of Lesbos. It was a society of high culture, of refined taste, of that ease of intercourse and freedom of manners which within its own narrow circle is the privilege and the grace of an aristocracy. Art could become unrestrainedly personal: for the artist wrote for him-

[1] Alcman, frag. 60.

self and his own circle. Where an aristocracy make their own poetry, instead of having it made for them by professional poets, the Homeric minstrels or mediaeval jongleurs, they have no temptation to write except about what really interests them. The themes of the epic cycle, the *κλέα ἀνδρῶν*, were what was conventionally supposed to interest them; the professional minstrel, bound alike by his social position and by the inherited tradition of his craft, kept within this limit, or did not venture far beyond it. That kind of poetry was outworn. In the personal note of the lyric, poetry found a new life. Hence the lyric, until in its turn it becomes patterned and conventional, has no defined scope of matter or treatment. Its free drift halts not particularly. Love or adventure or hunger, the beauty of nature, political antagonisms, whatever the lyric poet feels acutely, kindle in him and issue in a lyric note. The lyric follows instinct; and in the immense range and difference of instinct lies the range of lyric poetry, and the difference—the greatest of all differences in poetry—between the good lyric and the bad.

There is another difference almost as great: that between the true lyric and the false. This does not lie in a difference of emotional instinct, but in the difference between a real emotion and one which is secondary, induced, or simulated. As soon as the lyric has become a recognised literary form this danger sets in. First there is the secondary lyric, which rises out of a real emotion, but an emotion which, though real as far as it goes, is not powerful or keen enough to compel lyrical expression, but only to suggest it and to make an effort towards it. The result is not a pure lyric: it is helped out or patched up by the use of lyrical forms already in existence. Where there is a sound instinct, lyric poetry thus produced may be very good indeed, but it can never be the best; and between the good and the best in this as in all art the difference is infinite. Next, there is the lyric in which the emotion is second-hand, the emotion of literature as it may be called rather than the emotion of life. This type of poetry, the lyric of induced or derivative emotion, is familiar in all periods of literary culture. Lastly, there is the false lyric, not born of emotion at all, but the dexterous machine-made product of simulated emotion. It is not always possible to assign a particular poem to one of these kinds. Art is not so simple a thing as that; they merge into one another, even in the work of the same writer, even within the limits of the same poem. It is an easy thing to see that some poetry is essentially false or bad: it is no very difficult matter to see that some other poetry is essentially true or essentially good. But of most poetry, as of most art generally, neither the one thing nor the other can be said without qualification. Between the two extremes, we are always dealing with the product of an instinct more or less sound towards the method of expressing an emotion more or less direct and vital; and not only towards the method, but towards the limit of expression, and towards the hold on what is central in the complex tissue of emotion.

The fragments of Sappho leave us in no doubt as to her rank among lyric poets. Like the lyrical work of Catullus and Shelley, they are beyond criticism. A keenness of emotion unsurpassed by any poet takes form in them under the guidance of an instinct which seems never to fail. All praise of her poetry tends to become ecstatic and hyperbolical; but these are just the epithets that can never be applied to her poetry itself. Most attempts that have been made to reproduce it or to communicate its quality force the note: her own note is never forced. The simplest things that have been said about her are the truest. After all the pomp of words has been exhausted, we have to fall back, in one form or another, on the naïve but curiously true phrase used of her by Strabo, *θαυμαστόν τι χρῆμα*, "a marvellous creature."

Μεμιγμένα πυρὶ φθέγγεται, "her utterance is mingled with fire," an ancient author says of Sappho, in one of those incidental remarks which often hit nearer the mark than formal criticism; and it is curious to observe how constantly the metaphor of fire, in one form or another, recurs in all her eulogists. Yet it is inadequate and even misleading in what it suggests. In its ordinary acceptation it involves a misapprehension of Sappho's central poetical quality. Nothing is more remarkable in her work than a quality which the epithet "fiery" in its customary use certainly does not imply—a quality of straightforward, lucid, unadorned expression. Her fire is not a raging element; it is a steady lustre which does not scorch or dazzle, the brilliance of which is only realised when, turning our eyes away from it to other poetry, we find that other poetry dim by comparison. Her fire is cool, like that of a gem. While it is true that, in the phrase I have already quoted, the purple of other poets seems to turn ashen-coloured when laid beside hers, there is no poet from whom the purple patch is more conspicuously absent. Only in the very greatest poets, and in these when they are at their best, do we find this inexplicable and overwhelming simplicity, the outcome of faultless instinct acting on elemental emotion. It is the ultimate magic of art. We read a few simple words simply put together; we admire them and pass on; and then we find that there is some witchery in them that makes us go back, and again back, and yet again back, to make sure that we have not missed something, to try to find what it is in them that moves us so. We dilute and dilate them (the phrase is that of Swinburne in speaking of his own attempts to render the fragments of Sappho into English); we lavish our utmost resources on trying to express some mere fraction of the beauty we find in them; and in the end we find that we have merely blurred and confused what we have been trying to elucidate, that the magic and mystery still seem, as they seemed at first, just beyond our reach.

This elusive magic, while it is a quality of all

Sappho's poetry, is found in its most obvious form where the passion of love is the subject of the poetry. It is this by which, to the ancient as well as the modern world, she has been chiefly known. The accident through which the only two fragments of her poetry that reach beyond half-a-dozen lines in length —the hymn to Aphrodite and the so-called ode to Anactoria—are concerned directly with this passion, has tended to confirm the current view. But the fragments show clearly that the range of her lyre was much wider; and whatever the subject, all bear the same translucent quality, comparable to that of water and air as much as that of fire. "Now I will sing to my fellow-women delightful things," so one of the fragments runs; of the delightful things love was the first, but there were many others; and the Muses "who made me precious, giving me their own crafts," did not narrow their gift to the art of love.[1] One passage, the text of which is unfortunately ruinous, speaks of "my joy in the light of the sun holding within it all things radiant and fair."[2] One is a speech of delicate self-abasement, spoken with the effect of a catch in the voice and tears behind the eyes: "Surely I am not one of those who bear malice in their temper, but my heart is innocent."[3] One is a keen, swift flicker of woman's jealousy: "What country girl is this that bewitches your sense, one that does not know how to draw her skirts about her ankles?" Another is a wail against ingratitude: "Those harm me most by whom I have done well."[4]

[1] Fragg. 10, 11. [2] Frag. 79. [3] Frag. 72. [4] Fragg. 70, 12.

Of another we only know the substance as cited by Aristotle;[1] but even so we may gather that it expressed a profound reflection on human life in language of grave clear beauty: "Or as Sappho said, that death is evil; for the Gods have so judged; else they would have died."

Many deal with the loveliness of nature, as seen in "an isle under Ionian skies" where, as Herodotus says, "the climate and seasons are the most beautiful of any cities in the world we know." These pictures are incomparably vivid: the orchard in summer where "on both sides cool water tinkles through apple-boughs, and slumber floats down from rustling leaves;" the full moon shining, and the stars standing fixed as round an altar; a cloud of sparrows descending through the air in a whirl of wings; storm sweeping down the hill upon a roaring oakwood;[2] or those exquisite lines, the best known I suppose of all her work, about the apple that reddens on a top branch, atop of the topmost, and the apple-gatherers forgot it, no, did not forget it, but could not reach it—

οἶον τὸ γλυκύμαλον ἐρεύθεται ἄκρῳ ἐπ' ὔσδῳ,
ἄκρον ἐπ' ἀκροτάτῳ, λελάθοντο δὲ μαλοδρόπηες,
οὐ μὰν ἐκλελάθοντ' ἀλλ' οὐκ ἐδύναντ' ἐπίκεσθαι.

This last passage is an instance of the way in which Sappho's poetry has been sophisticated by modern sentiment, just as in later Greece it was defaced by Athenian vulgarity. One hardly knows whether to be more grateful to Rossetti for his beautiful transla-

[1] *Rhetoric*, ii. 23. [2] Fragg. 4, 53, 1, 42.

tion of these lines, or more annoyed with him for linking with them, and fixing in them almost irrevocably, a sentiment which does not belong to them, nor to the almost equally beautiful passage which they suggested to Catullus. It is one of the many instances which go to prove that poetry is untranslateable, because what the translator reproduces is not the original itself, but the original as limited by, or extended over, the emotional effect produced by it on his own mind.

Now with the Greek lyrists, and with Sappho preeminently, this emotional effect is so powerful that in translating it, as in criticising it, one almost inevitably not only dilates and dilutes but distorts it. Listen to the gorgeous rhetoric of Swinburne's *Anactoria*—

Yea, thou shalt be forgotten like spilt wine
Except these kisses of my lips on thine
Brand them with immortality ; but me—
Men shall not see bright fire nor hear the sea
Nor mix their hearts with music, nor behold
Cast forth of heaven with feet of awful gold
And plumeless wings that make the bright air blind
Lightning, with thunder for a hound behind
Hunting through fields unfurrowed and unsown—
But in the light and laughter, in the moan
And music, and in grasp of lip and hand
And shudder of water that makes felt on land
The immeasurable tremor of all the sea,
Memories shall mix and metaphors of me.

The secondary emotion in these lines is perfectly genuine; but it is secondary. The instinct is followed; but the instinct is not perfectly sound. *Μνάσεσθαί τινά φαμι καὶ ὕστερον ἄμμεων* are the words of Sappho herself: "I say that one shall remember me even afterward."[1] That one low, pellucid phrase is all.

Or take Swinburne again—for when he wrote his *Anactoria* he was little more than a boy—coming with trained power of expression and matured judgment to Sappho once more, coming as close to her as he can—

> *I loved thee*—hark, one tenderer note than all—
> *Atthis, of old time once*—one low long fall
> Sighing—one long low lovely loveless call
> Dying—one pause in song so flamelike fast—
> *Atthis, long since in old time overpast*—
> One soft first pause and last.

The emotion is not perhaps so real, but the instinct for expression is much truer. Yet how far and far away still from the Greek, how indistinct by comparison! *Ἠράμαν μὲν ἔγω σέθεν, Ἄτθι, πάλαι πότα*, "I loved you once, Atthis"[2]—just one sliding sigh and whisper of sound. Only one English poet has known the secret of this melody.

> —But what music?
> —My lord, I hear none.
> —None?
> The music of the spheres.

That might be said, I think, about Sappho: and it is said as Sappho might have said it.

To antiquity Sappho was "the poetess" as Homer was "the poet." She still remains so. Many women have written poetry, and some have written poetry of high merit and extreme beauty. But no other woman can claim an assured place in the first rank of poets.

[1] Frag. 32. [2] Frag. 33.

Among the Greek lyrists are the names of some half-dozen women who came in the catalogue of the lyric poets, howbeit they attained not unto the Nine: Corinna of Tanagra, the rival of Pindar and one of his most acute critics; Murtis of Anthedon and Telesilla of Argos; Erinna, that fascinating and elusive figure who somewhere and at some time—as to her country and her date all is uncertainty—died at nineteen, an inheritress of unfulfilled renown. Of these as of their successors in other ages and countries no one has stood by the side of the great Lesbian—

> *οὐδ' ἴαν δοκίμοιμι προσίδοισαν φάος ἀλίω*
> *ἔσσεσθαι σοφίαν πάρθενον εἰς οὐδένα πω χρόνον*
> *τοιαύταν.*

"Into all time I think no maiden that looks on the light of the sun shall be such in wisdom."[1]

It is not, to be sure, of herself that Sappho says this; though when every fragment in which a pronoun of the first person occurs is tortured into a piece of autobiography, this one might be thrown in with as much reason as others. For the quality of *σοφία*, "wisdom"—something that includes the more precise notions of culture, insight, and balance—is as characteristic of this marvellous creature as her flame-like passion and her faultless language. It was by this gift among the rest that the Muses made her precious. One famous passage is a condemnation to oblivion of some one—"an uneducated woman," says the collector who has preserved the lines—for lack of the wisdom that makes

[1] Frag. 69.

remembrance outlive death. "Sometime thou shalt lie dead, and no memory of thee shall be either then or afterward, for thou hast no part in roses from Pieria; but even in the chambers of Death thou shalt pass unknown flitting forth among the dim ghosts." That is the bare colourless English of her own gorgeously modulated choriambics—

κατθάνοισα δὲ κείσεαι πότα, κωὐ μναμοσύνα σέθεν
ἔσσετ' οὔτε τότ' οὔτ' ὕστερον, οὐ γὰρ πεδέχεις βρόδων
τῶν ἐκ Πιερίας, ἀλλ' ἀφάνης κἠν 'Αΐδα δόμοις
φοιτάσεις πεδ' ἀμαύρων νεκύων ἐκπεποταμένα.[1]

In these lines we may see clearly the high intellectual passion which is as remarkable in Sappho's work as the more sensuous passion through which she has her unique fame. The Love whom she saw, ἐλθόντ' ἐξ ὀράνω πορφυρίαν περθέμενον χλάμυν, "descending from heaven clad in purple vesture,"[2] is akin to the intellectual and spiritual love of Plato and of Dante.

Among the most beautiful of Provençal poems is an *alba* by a poetess of unknown name which might have been written by one of the scholars of Sappho. It is best known by its lovely and haunting refrain, the

Oy dieus! oy dieus! de l' alba tan tost ve!

which has something of the simplicity and poignancy of a line of Sappho's own. But the whole piece, though in a lower key and with far less accomplished workmanship, recalls that fresh early lyric impulse of the Aeolian poets. It has not the splendour and inevitableness of

[1] Frag. 68. [2] Frag. 64.

its Greek prototype, but it has a similar delicacy and sweetness, "la doss' aura qu' es venguda de lay."

En un vergier sotz fuelha d' albespi
Tenc la dompna son amic costa si.

Plagues a dieu ja la nueitz non falhis
Ni 'l mieus amicx lonc de mi no s partis.

Bels dous amicx, fassam un joc novel
Ins el jardi on chanton li auzel.

La dompna es agradans e plazens;
Per sa beautat la gardon mantas gens.

"In an orchard, under the hawthorn leaf, the lady holds her lover close to her. Might it please God the night would never wane, nor my love separate far from me. Fair sweet love, let us renew delight, in the garden where the birds sing. The lady is gracious and pleasant; many people regard her for her beauty. Ah, God! ah, God! the dawn fleets so soon!"

The analogies between the two civilisations and the two poetries which they produced as their flower are more than superficial and are in some ways wonderfully close. In both we have a cultured and very likely a dissolute governing class; a freedom allowed to women in life and speech which scandalised the rest of the world; poetry and music seriously studied by organised schools or guilds. The *hetairiai* of Lesbos, associations of women for the cultivation of poetry and music, have their nearest parallel in those Courts of Love which existed in Languedoc from the twelfth to the fourteenth century. We have lists of a number of these: the beautiful names, Elys, Béatrix, Héleine, Ermengarde, Azalais, are like those of Sappho's associates, Atthis and Andromeda, Cleïs and Anactoria and Gyrinno. Among them one, Estephanette de Gantelmes, is named as having had a prominent place, and a reputation in poetry something like Sappho's. "Il est vray," says Jean de Nostredame, quoting as his authority some one called the Monk of the Islands of Gold, "que Phanette ou Estephanette, comme três excellente en la poésie, avoit une fureur, ou inspiration divine, laquelle estoit estimée un vray don de Dieu."[1]

It may not be irrelevant to quote what Raynouard says, in his classical work on the Troubadour literature, as to the scope and influence of the lyric poetry of Provence, for much of it is strikingly applicable to the earlier lyric of Hellas. After tracing the development of the Romance language, the κοινή or common literary dialect of the western Mediterranean: "subjected," as he says, "to new combinations of poetry and versification, it was devoted by the Troubadours to expressing the delicacy and liveliness of love, the uncompromising outspokenness (la sévère franchise) of their moral and political opinions, their enthusiasm for noble deeds and for the illustrious persons who wrought them, their just and bold indignation against the errors and faults of their contemporaries; and then a new literature began."

"When we have studied," Raynouard adds, "and appreciated the substance and form of these com-

[1] *Vies des plus célèbres et anciens poètes provençaux*, 1575: cited by Raynouard, *Choix des Poésies des Troubadours*, vol. ii. p. xciv. foll. According to Nostredame, this Phanette was the aunt of the Laurette de Sade whom he identifies with Petrarch's Laura. But even Sade (*Mémoires pour la vie de Pétrarque*) had to admit reluctantly that Nostredame was an "auteur trop fabuleux."

positions, we must allow to these poets the talent and the glory of having created an independent kind of poetry, which has become for part of Europe the characteristic and fertile type of the beauties of feeling, imagery and expression."

But Provence, while it produced much lyric poetry of great delicacy and charm, does not seem ever to have produced a great lyric poet: and in the lyric even more than in other forms of poetry, the difference is vital between what is first-rate and what falls short of being first-rate. Its perfection depends on the finest balance between qualities which are always tending to pull against one another: finish of style and direct expression of feeling. In Sappho we have the finished style, the γλαφυρὸς χαρακτήρ of the Greek critics, to a degree in which they held her to excel all other lyric poets. Opinion may be divided as to this; but if not unequalled, she is at least unsurpassed in this quality. Alcaeus among her contemporaries, Ibycus among her successors, perhaps reach the same level, but so far as can be judged from the fragments, they do not apply their style to any material with the same unfaltering certainty. Early in the fifth century B.C. the secret of the style became lost.

The well-worn comparison of the nightingale, so constantly and inevitably applied to Sappho and her poetry, has a real value if it is not carelessly used. From these miraculous lines in the Odyssey, already quoted—

ὡς δ' ὅτε Πανδαρέου κούρη χλωρηῒς
ἀηδὼν καλὸν ἀείδῃσιν ἔαρος νέον ἱσταμένοιο—

Even as when the maid of Pandarus,
The greenwood nightingale melodious,
Amid the thickened leafage sits and sings
When the young spring is waxing over us;

And she with many a note and hurrying trill
Pours forth her liquid voice, lamenting still
Her own son Itylus, King Zethus' child,
Whom long ago her folly made her kill—

which are in fact a lyric fragment embedded in the epic structure, down to Keats's immortal ode, the distance is great. In the one we have the bird's song with all its flexible sweetness, profusion, unselfconsciousness; in the other we hear it through an atmosphere charged with thought, with romance, with the passion and mystery of life. In Sappho it is different from both. The nightingale-note with her is not so much the rapture that "feeds the heart of the night with fire," the passionate thronging of notes and the triumphant burst of song, as that low inward contralto which is beyond the reach of any other singer, and in its liquid piercing sweetness is by itself and alone. Sometimes it is tremulous as if it floated on an ebb of passion, like the voice of one who has sought and not found, and still seeks and is not satisfied: the *Ich liebe eine Blume, doch weiss ich nicht welche* of Heine.

Die Nachtigall schlägt, und ich verstehe
Den süssen Gesang.
Uns beiden ist so bang und wehe,
So weh und bang.

Sometimes it is simply clear and passionless; and here it is that Sappho reaches the absolute summit of the lyric. 'Αἰπάρθενος ἔσσομαι, "Maiden shall I be for ever"[1]: just these two words in their liquid beauty, their simple purity, might be the final epitaph on a poetry which with all its swift ardour and flame-like passion is at its inmost heart grave, delicate, almost virginally austere. It is this note that sounds in the two lines preserved from her last poem, addressed to her daughter from her death-bed—

ἀλλ' οὐ γὰρ θέμις ἐν μοισοπόλῳ οἰκίᾳ
θρῆνον ἔμμεναι· οὐκ ἄμμι πρέπει τάδε.

"It is not right that there be mourning in the house of poetry; this befits not us."[2] Into this grave, still music the fire and splendour of passion, the richness and beauty of song, have become absorbed and transmuted. It is the last note of the Muse of Lesbos.

[1] Frag. 96.
[2] Frag. 136.

II

THE AGE OF CONCENTRATION: SIMONIDES

In the later part of the sixth century B.C. a great change passed over Hellas. It put away childish things; the lovely, irresponsible period of adolescence was over. Under the pressure of a great world-movement in which it was the centre and the battle-ground, it drew itself together intellectually, knitted its nerves, concentrated and hardened. We see the Hellenic spirit no longer as that of a delicate maiden gathering flowers—ἄνθε' ἀμέργουσαν παῖδ' ἄγαν ἀπαλάν [1] —but rather like one of the awful figures of Michael Angelo, massive and brooding, tortured by an insatiable curiosity and a fierce desire of perfection. Greek poetry had still to make what are possibly its greatest achievements, but it made them through minds overburdened with thought, and eyes at once restless and piercing, which searched deep into the profound mysteries of life. In this poetry of fully developed Hellas the brain counts for more, the instinct for less. Sparta was becoming brutalised, and poetry there dwindled away. The large diffused Ionian culture narrowed upon Athens. The demand of the

[1] Sappho, frag. 121.

H

modern spirit was for action, and again action, and always action. The drama arose, and merged into itself the intellectualised elements of the lyric, on the larger plane towards which men's minds had been drawn by the rediscovery or reinstatement of the epic. Poetry ceased to be the natural flower of life: it became a weapon, exquisitely fine and keen, wielding the resources of a hitherto unknown science, and attempting, not without success, to become the imaginative function of a life tense, complex, and active beyond all previous experience.

Into this period fall the names of the last among the nine lyric poets of the canon. Between the birth of Simonides and the death of Pindar there is an interval of about one hundred years. Simonides, belonging by date of birth to an earlier generation, that of the island-poets who gathered from all quarters of the Hellenic world to the brilliant literary court of Samos, attained a great age, and wrote much of his finest poetry after the Persian wars. Pindar, born some forty years later, lived on to the time at which the Athenian empire began to break up. Bacchylides, the nephew of Simonides and the rival of Pindar, brings the series of the great lyric poets to a close just after the outbreak of the Peloponnesian war.

In this century, full of cross-currents and complex developments, it is not easy to trace any central clue, still less to fix any central figure in poetry. We seem to be watching not so much a steady movement of sunlight while the earth swings round upon her axis, as an electric storm full of flashes and sparkles, flame leaping suddenly from one point to another and as suddenly extinct.

There is indeed one remarkable figure whom it is impossible to pass over, even apart from the fact that we possess a fully representative body of his poetry. Pindar was unanimously placed by Greek judgment at the head of the lyric poets, and this estimate was confirmed by the lucid and unbiassed criticism of Quintilian. But he can hardly be called the central figure of his period. The only one of the nine who belongs to Greece Proper, he is in a way less Greek than the rest. He differs from all his contemporaries in seeming not to belong to his age. He is the one great poet produced by Thebes; and Thebes, then as always, stood curiously outside of Hellas. The separatist attitude taken up by Boeotia in the Persian wars is only the most incisive instance of an aloofness of temper which characterises it from first to last. Just as Thebes gives the feeling of being somehow outside of Hellas, Pindar gives the feeling of being somehow outside of Hellenic poetry. The finest modern critics are inconclusive about him; they praise him and make sudden reservations; they repeat one another, sometimes, as it would seem, mechanically and without full conviction. This is because, consciously or not, they are baffled by him. Under analysis, he becomes a mere string of contradictions. He is the most religious of the Greek poets; he was accepted as inspired by Delphi, and here and there gives utterance, in language of unexampled splendour, to the deepest religious emotions; yet his odes give the impression of one who worships nothing but worldly success and fame, unless it be high birth. He is a master of language, who seems to write whatever comes into his head. He affects us with an almost speechless admiration, and then, in a moment, leaves us floundering in a maze of tortured language about things that do not interest us. "Few people care for Pindar now," says Professor Murray in a single sharp sentence. It may be doubted whether many people ever cared for him, any more than he cared for them. *Tendit in altos nubium tractus,* says Horace of him; and indeed there is something about him meteoric, as of one whose poetry is barely human. At one moment, borne on by the rush of his language, we feel as if there was never any poetry like it; at another, we are merely dazzled and fatigued, and the impression he gives in the original (as he almost uniformly does in a translation) is of something grotesque and almost monstrous. The momentum of his poetry is perhaps unequalled. The science of his art never fails him. He handles great rhythmical masses with absolute mastery and precision. The lifting movement and great crash of sound in his odes are almost incredible in their magnitude; his instrument is an organ with all the stops out. But we ache in this whirl of sound for the *vox humana,* or a phrase of the lovely flute-stop that goes straight to the heart.

Of Pindar, then, as of few poets, it may be said that there is to him *nil simile aut secundum.* A personality so constituted never recurred, and all attempts to imitate it are foredoomed failures. He was created to show what might be done in art and not done a second time. One might perhaps without being over-fanciful draw an analogy between him and the only other great figure in the history of Thebes. Her two imperishable names are those of Pindar and Epaminondas. The two men came at times when the art of lyric poetry and the art of warfare had been developed and reduced to system; they revolutionised the practice of their arts by daring genius, that upset all established ideas. Take one of Pindar's great crashing phrases—one like the incomparable

> ἐκ δ' ἄρ' αὐτοῦ πομφόλυξαν δάκρυα γηραλέων
> γλεφάρων
> ἂν περὶ ψυχὰν ἐπεὶ γάθησεν ἐξαίρετον
> γόνον ἰδὼν κάλλιστον ἀνδρῶν.

I must reluctantly make an exception here to my rule of translating any Greek that I quote; for the essence of a phrase like this is just that it is untranslateable: the volume and splendour of sound in it *are* the poetry. Its impact is as irresistible as that of the wedged column of fifty shields in depth that rammed the flower of the Spartan army to wreck at Leuctra. But Leuctra set no fashion of tactics, and Pindar set no fashion of poetry; both remain dazzling and lonely achievements. A generation after Epaminondas, the art of war was put on a different footing by Alexander. Within Pindar's own lifetime, the central life of poetry passed away from the lyric. When the Theban general lay with the spear-head in his breast at Mantineia and was told that the wound was mortal, "Then," he said, "you must make peace." Pindar's last word might have been similar: "Then you must close the roll of the lyric poets." There was nothing else to be done: τὸ πόρσω δ' ἔστι σοφοῖς ἄβατον κἀσόφοις· οὐ μὴ διώξω· κεινὸς εἴην—"For the wise and the simple alike the path leads no further: I will not pursue it: it were in vain."[1]

I quoted just now a phrase from a poem of Meredith's, in which, as in much of his poetry, there seems to me to be something more nearly approaching the manner of Pindar than in the work of any other modern poet. Both, in the words of the admirable criticism by Corinna upon Pindar, "sow not with the hand, but with the whole sack." As regards insight into life and power of thought they of course stand far apart. But they are akin in their dazzling use of language, in the intricacy and splendour of their orchestration, as well as in their swift transitions and violent metaphors, continually verging on the grotesque but saved by a sublime self-confidence. Let me quote from this same poem in illustration. It is not written in elaborate and involved metres like those of the formal Ode, such as he uses, for instance, in the *Odes in Contribution to the Song of French History*: it is in regular stanzas of simple construction; but this makes its essentially Pindaric quality in evolution of thought and use of diction the more striking.

> With shudders chill as aconite
> The couchant chewer of the cud
> Will start at times in pussy fright
> Before the dogs, when reads her sprite
> The streaks predicting streams of blood.

---

[1] Pindar, *Olymp.* iii. 45.

That is Pindar all over. Pindar all over too is the end of the piece with its long ascending movement and final crash of sound—

> Should they once deem our emblem Pard
> Wagger of tail for all save war,
>
> Mechanically screwed to flail
> His flanks by Presses conjuring fear ;
> A money-bag with head and tail ;—
> Too late may valour then avail !
> As you beheld, my cannonier,
>
> When with the staff of Benedek
> On the plateau of Königgrätz
> You saw below that wedging speck,
> Foresaw proud Austria rammed to wreck
> Where Chlum drove deep in smoky jets.

Βούλομαι ἐμαυτῷ ζῆν, οὐκ ἄλλῳ, "I mean to live for myself, not for some one else," were, according to Eustathius, the scornful words flung by Pindar at Simonides. They express at once his strength and his weakness. He will be no man's servant; neither will he be the servant of any cause. At a time when the great flush of patriotism passed over Hellas, he walked among his dreams and his music, self-absorbed and alone. Salamis and Plataea are incidents he just deigns to notice, while he breaks into a passion of rapture over the victories of style: "The thing that one says well goes forth with a voice unto everlasting." This attitude he imposed upon his contemporaries by the sheer mass and splendour of his genius. For the Athenian democracy he can have felt nothing but a distant contempt; it is the λάβρος στρατός, the "horde," of the second Pythian. Yet when for once he dipped his hand into the sack and flung to Athens, "like wealthy men who care not how they give," that string of gorgeous epithets that flash like jewels, "O shining, violet-crowned, song-famed, illustrious town," they were greedily accepted as though a gift from some god's hand, and taken by Athens for her motto through all the ages. Poetry to him moved among things greater than these; why his poetry is so perplexing and in the end so unsatisfying is that some of the things he cares about seem really great, and others quite infinitesimally small.

> ἐπάμεροι· τί δέ τις; τί δ' οὔ τις; σκιᾶς ὄναρ
> ἄνθρωπος· ἀλλ' ὅταν αἴγλα διόσδοτος ἔλθῃ
> λαμπρὸν φέγγος ἔπεστιν ἀνδρῶν καὶ μείλιχος αἰών.

"Things of a day, what are we and what are we not? The dream of a shadow is humankind; yet when a god-given splendour falls, light shines radiant upon men and life is sweet."[1] So he says at a thrilling height of rapt emotion; and then, apparently with the same thrill, he will speak of a horse-race or a dinner-party as though these things too were at the heart of life. Above all, we miss in him tears and laughter; all the common and dear emotions are left untouched by him, and seemingly left him untouched. He is one of those great poets—they include some of the greatest—who are without love and without pity.

The qualities which are absent in Pindar are just those which are conspicuous in Simonides. If not the greatest among the Greek lyrists—and in certain specific

[1] *Pyth.* viii. 95–7.

lyrical qualities five at least out of the nine may claim to excel him—he is the most broadly and nobly Hellenic. He is distinguished beyond all the rest by Greek refinement. All his work has a tempered dignity and suavity, combined with that specific quality of tenderness which makes him a spirit akin to Virgil. His genius seems to have been one of those which mature slowly and require length of life for their full development. In this respect he presents an interesting parallel with Sophocles. Both lived into their ninetieth year, and both did their finest work in poetry after an age at which the springs of poetry have in most men run dry. Both represent, more fully than any other among the generations of poets with whom they were contemporary, the whole life and progress of poetry during their own age; and the one hundred and fifty years over which their joint lives extend are a period which, taking it for all in all, is the most wonderful in human history. Both give in poetry the Hellenic temper at its finest and fullest; its sanity, its culture, its patriotism, its large, grave, temperate handling of life. To both the double-edged epithet of faultless may be attached without implying the note of depreciation which the word often is meant to convey.

Simonides is the last of the great island poets. Ionian culture is now flooding back to concentrate in Athens. The brilliant constellation of the Lesbian and Samian poets had set. Ceos, his birthplace, is only divided by a few miles of sea from Sunium, and is almost an outlying fragment of Attica. The Asiatic influences which helped to mould the civilisation of the larger and richer islands off the Ionian coast did not reach over to it; it breathed the thin clear air of Greece. Alone among the Cyclades, Ceos sent its little fleet, two triremes and two fifty-oared galleys, to fight against the Persians at Artemisium. According to legend, it was the fragment of a larger island, four-fifths of which had sunk under the sea, and a touch of mystery and sanctity still clung about it. Poetry and music were hereditary arts in the family of Simonides. It was as a trained poet of recognised distinction that he left his native island for the court of the Peisistratids. The rest of his life was mainly spent at Athens. There was an interlude of some years in Thessaly, spent among the castles of the feudal nobility; and the last years of his old age were passed at Syracuse, where the splendid court of Hiero welcomed him, together with Pindar and Aeschylus. But broadly speaking, we may call him not only the link between Ionia and Athens, but the first of the great Athenian poets.

In what survives of his lyrics likewise we feel already the specific Athenian tone. They have the quality which made Athens, from the time of the Persian wars onward, the heart and brain of the Greek world, "the Hellas of Hellas" in the striking phrase attributed to Thucydides. In becoming Athenian, Greek poetry both gained and lost. But both in the loss and in the gain it became more intensely Greek. It parted finally with romance. The piercing sweetness of the earlier lyric passed away: its lovely childishness and delicate magic were not for that age of dust and sweat. Political and ethical thought were filling three-fourths of life. The human intellect was for the first time feeling and exercising all its powers. Poetry answered to the demands of life; it became intellectualised; it grew fine, a little hard, like a stripped athlete trained down to the last ounce: when at its best, it is a miracle; missing its best, if but by the difference of a hair-breadth, it is hardly poetry at all.

The invention of prose had the effect on poetry not only of delimiting its province, but of laying on it new, stringent, and it might almost seem impossible requirements. Just at the time when it was becoming more and more a vehicle of thought, it found itself faced by and forced into rivalry with a new art designed to express thought directly. The demand was made of it, while remaining poetry, to do the work of prose. It did this; but at a great cost. On the one hand, it ran the constant risk of becoming prosaic. In the effort to save itself from this danger it incurred another, that of being consciously and artificially poetical. *Λεπτὰ δ' ἄταρπος, νηλεὴς δ' ἀνάγκα· εἰ δὲ λέγει τις ἄλλως, πλατεῖα κέλευθος*—"Narrow is the path, merciless the necessity, but broad is the road for him who speaks amiss."[1] Simonides treads that narrow path with a sure foot, Pindar (if the traditional interpretation of his words is correct) spoke with contempt of his rival's poetry as an art that could be learned, as uninspired and mechanical. The same criticism has been made on the Odes of Horace. It will be time enough to consider its relevance when the mechanism has been

[1] Alcman, frag. 81; Bacchylides, frag. 37.

mastered, when any one learns, or can teach, the art of producing poetry like theirs. At whatever point we draw the line between art and inspiration, the grave beauty and noble tenderness of Simonides, even more than his faultless grace and finish, are what give him his place among the master-poets.

That place indeed has, but for the attack of Pindar, never been seriously challenged. His reputation in his own lifetime was immense and almost universal. The very mythology which grew round his name, as it did round those of all the great poets, took a colour from the quality of his genius. The legends about Pindar are fantastic and extravagant: bees swarmed about his lips at Thespiae; he heard the god Pan singing one of his own hymns. Those about Simonides have a peculiar refinement and gravity like his own grave and refined poetry. He lived under a special divine care and guardianship.

> I find it written of Simonides,
> That, travelling in strange countries, once he found
> A corpse that lay exposed upon the ground,
> For which, with pains, he caused due obsequies
> To be performed, and paid all holy fees.
> Soon after this man's ghost unto him came,
> And told him not to sail, as was his aim,
> On board a ship then ready for the seas.
> Simonides, admonished by the ghost,
> Remained behind: the ship the following day
> Set sail, was wrecked, and all on board were lost.
> Thus was the tenderest Poet that could be,
> Who sang in ancient Greece his moving lay,
> Saved out of many by his piety.

So Wordsworth wrote, at the time which was the culminating period of his poetry. I have quoted the sonnet in full, partly because the authentic text of 1803 has never hitherto been correctly reprinted, but also because it shows, even better than other more widely known passages, the strong attraction that the one poet exercised over the other; and because, like a good deal of Wordsworth's finest work, it is written in something very near to the Simonidean manner. In both there is the same simple gravity and delicacy, the same absence of any apparent effort, the same lucid straightforwardness that is almost like that of prose—"like, but ah, how different!" But the Greek Wordsworth, more fortunate than his English successor, carried the divine favour through life. His fame was not deferred to his old age; and in his old age the stream of poetry still issued with the same limpid melody, the same clear beauty.

Yet as he outlived his own generation, so he outlived the summer-time of the Greek lyric. In the still beauty of some of the fragments there is an autumnal quality, as of one of those golden days that carry the first message of the year's decay. "Who that is wise in mind," he says, "would praise Cleobulus the dweller in Lindus, who set the might of a pillar in rivalry with the ever-flowing rivers, and the spring flowers, and the golden flame of the sun and the shining moon and the eddies of the sea? For all things are subject to the Gods; and as for a stone, even the hands of mortals shatter it. Behold here the thought of a foolish man."[1] Not marble nor the gilded monuments of princes shall outlive this powerful

[1] Frag. 57.

rhyme; but to poetry also, as to the monument, decay comes in the end; the hands of mortals, as they have built it up, pull it down, and all things are subject to the Gods. In the poetry of Simonides there is that settled perfection at which poetry only stays for a little while before she girds herself for a fresh journey. Ἁ Μοῖσα ἐπέρχεται πάντα θεριζομένα, as he says in another passage; μή μοι καταπαύετε—"The Muse moves onward, gathering all things to her harvest; prithee stay her not."[1] Stay her not; no, the attempt would be idle, for she will not stay. He more than once takes the tone of a poet of the older generation, looking with doubtful eyes on the new art, the work of younger and slighter poets. It had not the old potency: κούρων δ' ἐξελέγχει νέος οἶνος οὐ τὸ πέρυσι δῶρον ἀμπέλου—"the new wine of boys puts not to shame last year's gift of the vine."[2] The allusion is said to be to an ode of Pindar's, in which he claimed precedence for "the flower of newer songs." It would apply equally to the poetry of his own kinsman, Bacchylides, that thinner and less generous vintage which was the last product of the waning lyric impulse.

Throughout his own work there is that perfect and seemingly spontaneous balance of thought and expression which makes great literature. But we may distinguish in it two sides of the higher and more intimate quality which makes great poetry; or rather, I should say, a union in markedly different proportions of two qualities. In his tenderer poetry he is not weak; in his stronger poetry he is not hard; but the harmony

[1] Frag. 46. [2] Frag. 75.

is variously compounded. From the pieces of the latter class we should not know that we were dealing with a poet of unsurpassed sweetness; from those of the former we should hardly know that we were dealing with a poet of unsurpassed dignity and elevation.

The famous Danaë fragment (37) is the finest surviving example of the tenderness of Simonides; the delicacy of phrasing, the refinement of diction, is in it applied to a subject of eternal beauty and pathos. For that picture of the baby, unconscious of night and storm and danger, asleep in its mother's arms, "cheek against cheek," *πρόσωπον κλιθὲν προσώπῳ*, while she whispers above it words that have nothing in them but love and sweet submission to God's will, there is no parallel in pre-Christian art; it is the first, and among the most perfect, of those pictures of the Virgin and Child which hold a central place in the love and awed admiration of mankind. The same exquisite delicacy, "a soft and solemn-breathing sound" that rises "like a stream of rich-distilled perfume," is shown in other fragments: we may note especially three. One is the passage describing, or rather embodying, for the picture is conveyed without a word of distinct description, the winter-calm of the days of the halcyon.

> *ὡς ὁπόταν χειμέριον κατὰ μῆνα πινύσκῃ*
> *Ζεὺς ἅματα τέσσαρα καὶ δέκα,*
> *λαθάνεμόν τέ μιν ὥραν καλέοισιν ἐπιχθόνιοι*
> *ἱρὰν παιδοτρόφον ποικίλας*
> *ἀλκυόνος.*[1]

---

[1] Frag. 12.

It is as wonderful an anticipation of the poetry of Christmas-tide (as you have it for instance in the speech of Marcellus in the opening scene of *Hamlet*) as the Danaë is of the poetry of the Nativity. The two others have not this note of strange magic; they are purely Hellenic in their import, and are distinguished from the work of the other lyric poets not by their feeling, but by the peculiar and indefinable charm of expression. If I quote them in English, it must be with the warning that no translation can give their specific quality, or make it clear how essential and how subtle is the difference between them and the passages from other Greek poets that treat of similar motives. One is the fragment (36) beginning, *οὐδὲ γὰρ οἳ πρότερόν ποτ᾽ ἐπέλοντο*—"For not even they who were earlier, and were half divine sons of royal gods, not even they fulfilled their life and reached old age without toil, without wasting, without peril." The motive is like that of a celebrated passage in Pindar's third Pythian—

αἰὼν δ᾽ ἀσφαλὴς
οὐκ ἔγεντ᾽ οὔτ᾽ Αἰακίδᾳ παρὰ Πηλεῖ—

"Secure life befel not either Peleus son of Aeacus or divine Cadmus: yet they of mortals are said to have reached the top of happiness, they who heard the gold-frontleted Muses singing on the mountain and in seven-gated Thebes, when the one wedded great-eyed Harmonia, and the one noble Thetis, child of Nereus the well-counselling." This passage is so fine that it was chosen, as you may remember, by Arnold for an instance of the evolution of genuine poetry. It is radiant and magnificent as only Pindar's best work is: yet when we turn from it to the still music of the other, it is Simonides who seems to be the finer artist. So likewise in the other fragment (53), the description of Meleager, "who outdid all young men with the spear, casting it over eddying Anaurus out of Iolcos rich in vines." The lines at once recall another hero, the half-shod man who crossed Anaurus, and the gorgeous central movement of the fourth Pythian; and on senses half stunned by the torrent of Pindar's music, the low clear note of Simonides seems to come, in its delicate perfection, as a symbol of what is most vital, and most unapproachable, in Greek poetry.

In the other type which we find among the great fragments of Simonides there is a more matured gravity, a more exalted but equally restrained passion. They are the poetry of thought made luminous by emotion, rather than of emotion controlled by thought. Such, for instance, is the Simonidean rendering of the line which in the earliest Greek poetry of reflection had said that "the gods lay sweat in front of virtue." "There is a tale that Virtue once dwelt on cliffs hard to climb, but now inhabits the holy place of gods and meets not the eyes of mortals visibly, save him on whom comes bitter inward sweat and who climbs to the top of manhood."[1] To this type too belongs the noble fragment of a threne on the dead at Thermopylae: "Whose fortune is glorious, and fair their doom, whose tomb is an altar, and for lamentation they have remembrance, and for pity, praise; and

[1] Frag. 58.

such a monument neither rust nor all-conquering Time shall make dim."[1]

In this passage, with its stately beauty, is the first foreshadowing of the transition. We hear in it, for the first time in literature, low down as it were under the poetry, the tone of Attic prose. In some of the later fragments of the Simonidean lyric this tone recurs more unmistakeably. Lyric poetry is becoming used for a purpose beyond itself. The springs of feeling are being diverted into the dry channel of thought, and used to turn wheels of the intellect. In the long passage of reflective and almost argumentative verse which is quoted and commented on in Plato's *Protagoras*, one sees the lyric ode as a thing that has fulfilled its function and will by-and-bye become obsolete. One sees the end coming still more clearly in another fragment (70), if it may be accepted as authentic on the shaky testimony of Sextus Empiricus *adversus Mathematicos*—

οὐδὲ καλᾶς σοφίας ἐστὶν χάρις
εἰ μή τις ἔχει σεμνὰν ὑγίειαν.

"There is no charm in beauteous wisdom unless one has venerable health." It sounds like an intentional parody. You have the thing full-blown in the *Paean to Health* by Ariphron of Sicyon, an otherwise unknown writer. "Health, most honoured of deities, may I dwell with thee for what remains of life and mayest thou be my willing housemate"—so it begins, and it goes on at the same level. It is the bastard lyric,

[1] Frag. 4.

such as desolated our own poetry in the eighteenth century. "Hail, Solitude, romantic maid"—every one knows the kind of thing. This was the downward path that lyric poetry took in Greece. It rapidly became formal and scholastic. On the one hand it lost itself in a barren wilderness of abstractions; on the other it developed into that gaudy and tumid rhetoric which has since then been almost inseparably associated with the name of the dithyramb. When Aristotle wrote his Poetics, the term *διθυραμβοποιητική* had come to be used pretty much in the sense of lyric poetry generally; and the final decadence was reached in the hands of the dithyrambist Timotheus, who was born in the year of the death of Pindar:

> So quick bright things come to confusion.

Timotheus represents the corruption of the lyric. His enormous popularity, which lasted long after his death, was the popularity that attaches, in all ages, to work that is showy, arrogant, and insincere. A famous fragment expresses his attitude towards art—

> οὐκ ἀείδω τὰ παλαιά,
> καινὰ γὰρ μάλα κρείσσω·
> νέος ὁ Ζεὺς βασιλεύει
> τὸ πάλαι δ' ἦν Κρόνος ἄρχων·
> ἀπίτω Μοῦσα παλαιά.

"I sing not the old songs, for the new are far better. Zeus is the new king where Cronos was lord of old; let the old Muse begone."[1] In their jaunty arrogance—even the rhythm in the original has a distinct touch of vulgarity—these lines are a strange contrast to

[1] Athenaeus, iii. 122 D.

the flutings of the earlier lyric, when poetry was full of the joy and eagerness of its youth, and the new songs were something fresh and divine. Set them beside the lovely invocation of Alcman—

> Μῶσ' ἄγε, Μῶσα λίγεια πολυμμελὲς
> αἰενάοιδε μέλος
> νεοχμὸν ἄρχε παρσένοις ἀείδεν—

"Muse, clear-voiced Muse, singer for ever, come, begin a new song, a song manifold, for maidens to sing,"[1] and you have the whole difference between a new-born and a dying art. It is a reflection and symbol of the change that had passed over Greek life. At an interval of three hundred years, Terpander and Timotheus took their new music and new poetry to Sparta. The lyre of seven strings brought with him by Terpander to the Dorian city was the accompaniment to a new poetry, of hitherto unknown range, freshness, and flexibility; and both were welcomed in the Sparta of those early times, then the centre of the simple and high Hellenic culture,

> ἔνθ' αἰχμά τε νέων θάλλει καὶ μῶσα λίγεια
> καὶ δίκα εὐρυάγυια—

"where blooms the spear of young warriors, and the clear-voiced Muse, and righteousness in the broad streets."[2] Timotheus brought his new eleven-stringed lyre and his florid modern poetry to a Sparta where iron military discipline was the one virtue left. In all else, glory and loveliness had passed away. The

[1] Frag. 1.

[2] Terpander, frag. 6.

life of poetry, like the life of the state, had lost the principle of growth. Conservatism was the only refuge from anarchy. The Spartan ephor who cut the strings away from the lyre of Timotheus is the concrete symbol of an age which, finding its own art debased or dead, vainly tries to go on living on the art of the past. It was the breaking of the white staves over the grave of Greek lyric poetry.

But long before this, lyric poetry had been undergoing that differentiation of function which is the sign that life is about to develop new forms. Simonides is not only one of the greatest, and perhaps the most fully representative of the Greek lyrists, but the greatest of the Greek epigrammatists.

The consideration of the epigram only belongs to a study of the Greek lyric in so far as the epigram embodied lyrical qualities and drew into itself part of the lyric impulse. It had been a form used not only by the elegists, but on occasion by the melic poets also—by Sappho, for instance, and by Anacreon. Simonides gave it a fresh life, a new amplitude and dignity; in his hands it assumed a poetical importance co-ordinate with that of the Ode. How nearly the spirit of the two distinct poetical forms approximates with him is obvious from instances where he has used both forms upon the same subject. The splendid fragment of his Ode on the heroes of Thermopylae, to which I have already made reference, is hardly distinguishable, except in metrical form, from those epitaphs on the saviours of Greece which are the most famous of his writings. These epigrams, and others of his, reach not only the highest level in their kind, but a point beyond which it seems inconceivable that art can go. As faultless in form as they are noble in thought and profound in their restrained feeling, they are among the perfect things in poetry. At that height and tension all poetry tends to merge in the lyric; for the lyric in its vital quality might almost be defined as that poetry in which, as in music, form and substance coalesce, and the thought becomes indistinguishable from the emotion.

The nearest analogy to this in English poetry is the sonnet. In the *Golden Treasury of the best Songs and Lyrical Poems in the English Language*—that is its full title—my predecessor Francis Palgrave included without hesitation a large number of sonnets among the pieces which conform more strictly to a technical definition of the lyric. Sonnets form about one-fifth of the whole number of poems in that collection—I speak of the volume as originally published—and I suppose no one has ever felt that they are out of tone with the other poems or that they impair the lyrical quality of the collection. But they are in any case only lyrics with a difference. It is worth noticing, though it is not a point on which stress can be laid, that they lack both of the two formal qualities distinctive of lyric poetry according to the Greek definition—the strophic construction and the mixed musical time. The chief masters of the sonnet in England have been the poets in whom, as with Wordsworth, the reflective outweighed the emotional instinct, or, as with Shakespeare and Milton, both lyric and sonnet were but interludes in larger and more sustained work. In Rossetti again we have a poet of essentially lyrical genius who, being attracted towards the sonnet-form for particular reasons, set himself deliberately to alter its scope and function, and forced into it a lyrical quality almost beyond what it will bear. Such an attempt in itself shows a certain defect, a certain want of sureness and soundness in the lyrical instinct.

Simonides has this instinctive certainty. The importance which he gave to the epigram is just what was exactly right at a time when a change was coming over the genius of the lyric. It was becoming quieter, more reflective, tending more towards composition and balance. If these new qualities were to gain a little more preponderance, the emotional impulse that gave it life would flag; it would slacken or stiffen. The secret of an earlier age was already lost; the white-hot precision, the passionate lucidity of Sappho was a thing past and irrecoverable. But the Simonidean epigram, in its brevity and high simplicity, was the instinctive recoil of poetry from a counter-movement of the lyric towards diffuseness, magniloquence, or sentimentality.

One of the best epigrams of Simonides is as straightforward and as unadorned as one of the great stanzas of Sappho. If we ask which is the greater achievement, the answer is that there is no answer, that they are not comparable, because no common measure can be applied to them. Each is in its kind perfect. One point I may just notice which is common to both poets: it is this, that they have ornament of the utmost richness and splendour at their disposal and control, and that the sparing use they make of it is a matter of deliberate choice and judgment, or, if we prefer to say so, a matter of unerring instinct. Some of the lighter, more fanciful fragments of Sappho are as thick-strung with glittering, ringing ornament as a fragment of Pindar; when she is writing straight from the heart there is hardly an epithet or a figure: πολὺ πάκτιδος ἀδυμελεστέρα, χρύσω χρυσοτέρα, "far sweeter-sounding than the harp, more gold than gold," she never thinks of gilding her gold or making music for her music. And so it is analogously with the very different art of Simonides. In those epigrams which are at a lower tension the ornament is rich and even splendid. Take his lines on a dead Thessalian hound, where, whether to please some wealthy sportsman or from a touch of his own tenderness reaching towards a four-footed creature he may have loved, he bent his august style to a slight subject—

Ἦ σεῦ καὶ φθιμένας λεύκ' ὀστέα τῷδ' ἐνὶ τύμβῳ
 ἴσκω ἔτι τρομέειν θῆρας, ἀγρῶσσι Λυκάς·
τὰν δ' ἀρετὰν οἶδεν μέγα Πήλιον, ἅ τ' ἀρίδηλος
 Ὄσσα, Κιθαιρῶνός τ' οἰονόμοι σκοπιαί.

"Surely even as thou liest dead in this tomb I deem the wild beasts yet tremble at thy white bones, O huntress Lycas; and thy virtue vast Pelion knows, and splendid Ossa and the lonely peaks of Cithaeron." The pomp of names and splendour of epithet are almost like Pindar. But when he is dealing with a subject that moves him most profoundly, with a great heroism or with the majesty of death, the ornament disappears; the language becomes simple, severe, almost bare.

Ὦ ξεῖν' ἄγγειλον Λακεδαιμονίοις ὅτι τῇδε
κείμεθα τοῖς κείνων ῥήμασι πειθόμενοι.

"O stranger, tell the Lacedaemonians that we lie here obeying their orders."

Κρὴς γενεὰν Βρόταχος Γορτύνιος ἐνθάδε κεῖμαι
οὐ κατὰ τοῦτ' ἐλθών, ἀλλὰ κατ' ἐμπορίαν.

"I, Brotachus of Gortyna, a Cretan, lie here, not having come hither for this, but for merchandise." Prose could not be simpler, quieter, more precise. We seem to hear nature herself speaking, as one who does not need to raise her voice.

This perfect taste and certainty in the use of language would no doubt be sufficient, in an age when language was almost worshipped, to give Simonides the reputation he had not only of a great poet, but of a great sage. His casual talk seems to have been treasured: there were collections of his apophthegms: if we may think of him as in some ways like a Greek Wordsworth, we might in this view rather call him a Greek Goethe. It is curious that against him as against Goethe and Wordsworth the charge of worldliness and selfishness was made, as it has been made rightly or wrongly against others in whom sanity was no less conspicuous than genius. Some sort of contrast or discrepancy seems to be felt between their tranquil and successful life and the lofty idealism of their art. Simonides got the reputation, like Wordsworth, of having a keen eye on the main chance, and, like Goethe, of loving ease and wealth and rank overmuch. He was accused of flattering his rich, high-born patrons, and of writing for money. He was the first poet, it is said, "to write for hire." Whatever that means, and however it is meant to discriminate his practice from that of the epic minstrels or of his own lyric predecessors, it probably only amounts to this, that among his other qualities he was an excellent man of business, and ordered his life prudently and successfully. In a dubious as well as in a transcendental sense of the words, a man of this type of genius may overcome the world. Perhaps in some of his lyrics, as in those of Goethe, there is just a suspicion of this worldly strain in the poet's temperament. Perfect in grace and accomplishment, thoughtful, melodious, dignified, they have a sort of reserve, like that of a wealthy man who does care how he gives, and who does not forget himself even for the love of his art. In any case, he and Pindar are both among the immortals.

But amongst the poets at the brilliant court of Syracuse there were not two immortals, but three: and the third was the greatest. Γαδείρων τὸ πρὸς ζόφον οὐ περατόν, "westward beyond Cadiz no man may pass," Pindar had said, in his haughty claim to have consummated the lyric. Already when these words were written Athens had heard a new thunder as of the whole Atlantic. The Aeschylean drama swept the lyric into the tide of a vaster movement. "The harp-strings have begun to cry out to the eagles."

THE note of the fifth century before Christ is that throughout it Athens is Greece. Politically, from the Persian wars onwards, Greek history is in this period the history of Athens and the Athenian empire. Athens is the focus upon which the whole movement of the Greek world converges, or from which it radiates The history and politics of all the other states of the Hellenic world can be mainly expressed in terms of their relations to Athens, whether of sympathy, or of antagonism and reaction.

So it is also in poetry. The poetic movement, so widely diffused in the lyric age of the seventh and sixth centuries, concentrates and fines down. Athens had already, in some way which for want of detailed evidence we cannot clearly explain, got hold of the epic; so much is the effective meaning of that movement in the history of the Homeric poems which is described or symbolised under the name of the Peisistratean recension. Whatever it was, it made Athens the Panionion, and even more than that, the Panhellenion of poetry. About a generation later, as part of the same movement, towards the end of the sixth century, lyric poetry had also converged on Athens. Simonides of Ceos is still one of the island poets, but not in the same sense as his predecessors, the schools of Lesbos or Teos, or that which gathered round the Samian court of Polycrates. He became, to all intents and purposes, an Athenian poet. The islands themselves had before his death become part of the Athenian empire. Pindar left no successor in poetry at Thebes. Sparta, once the home of a poetry unsurpassed in purity and delicacy, had fallen dumb; that unwalled city, from which no woman had ever seen the smoke of an enemy's camp-fire, was cut off by impenetrable barriers from movements of the spirit. Even Sicily was swept into the great movement of unification, and the Greater Greece beyond the seas became intellectually a suburb of Athens. "His country was the Hellas of Hellas, Athens," is the phrase, no less true than pointed, used in the famous epitaph on Euripides.

Athens was Greece, and Attic poetry was the drama. Almost at the same time when the ancient stock of the epic put forth a last shoot in the *Heracleid* written by the uncle of Herodotus, almost at the same time when the lyric reached its last development in the hands of Pindar and Simonides, the new dramatic poetry, the specific creation of Athens, was winning its first triumphs in the work of Chionides and Phrynichus. It came to conquer. There is no poet even of the second rank, except the dramatists, for the rest of the period of the ascendancy of Athens, after the roll of the lyrists closes with Bacchylides. Throughout the fifth century we may observe a double process going on; an expansion of the range, scope, and power of the drama, side by side with a contraction of the art and methods of poetry in general. The drama annexed poetry. Poetry was absorbed in the drama. Both tendencies went on accumulating. Both were functions of the central Hellenic instinct, the instinct which fulfilled itself wholly in Athens of the fifth century for the first and last time in human history. It culminated in Periclean Athens, and then flickered, flared, and collapsed. But by that time it had wrought itself indelibly into the Greek consciousness. Even in its actual ruin it remained a dominant and tyrannous ideal. Neither with it nor without it was life endurable. It essayed and all but effected impossibilities: and when it collapsed, it left life empty. Athens survived, a ghost of herself; there was even a phantom of a second Athenian empire. But the angel of Athens was a watcher by an empty tomb. Life and poetry had passed on, to transmute themselves, to prepare for fresh incarnations. No great new force arises in history until Philip and Alexander. No great new movement arises in poetry until the Alexandrians.

Attic poetry is the drama; and the Attic drama is Sophocles: for Sophocles is the single poet who embodies centrally and completely the spirit of Athens. Aeschylus may be a greater poet, if among poets of the first rank one may speak of greater and less, classifying the immortals and assigning places in the Olympian hierarchy. But he was more than Athenian; he was more than Greek. Euripides, an inferior artist, was a more potent and mordant intellect, a greater influence over life and letters. But in him the Athenian genius was transforming itself and preparing a new world; it is not without curious significance that he died in Macedonia. In Sophocles, and in him alone, we have Athenian poetry in its full expression, neither less nor more. He did in poetry what Athens of the fifth century tried to do in the whole field of life; and he did it so perfectly that he eludes all but the finest and most sensitive criticism, and remains to us something almost intangible and impersonal.

Athenian art is Greek art at its central point and highest power. Homer is pre-Hellenic; he is the inheritance which Hellas received from a great mediaeval past, and which moulded the whole of Greek poetry, as he was himself moulded subtly and yet vitally by the Greek spirit into something almost Greek. Passed through the Greek mind, the Homeric poems become insensibly, almost unconsciously, Hellenised. The lyric poets of the seventh and sixth centuries are Greek poetry in the making, in the *splendori antelucani*, the radiance and flushings of dawn. Now the sun was fully risen; and a mature art set itself, in the clear daylight, to express, embody, and interpret life.

This central Greek art of Athens, as we see it in the work of Pheidias or Ictinus or Sophocles, is something beyond all example clear, pure, and refined. It was the product of extraordinarily acute senses and wonderfully trained intelligence. To senses less acute, or to an intelligence less trained, it seems almost abstract, as though it were on the point of becoming disembodied. It has the thinness, one might say the dryness and rarefied quality, of the Attic air. The architecture and sculpture of that period are incredibly fine, and curiously reserved. They reach the utmost limits in subtlety of composition, purity of line, and delicacy of modelling. That art was content with nothing short of the highest achievement in the most difficult manner. To attain that end, it rejects or dispenses with anything that might hinder it. Its embodiment of life is so nearly abstract that any failure means complete failure; it stakes everything on this one cast. We may see this most clearly perhaps by studying the metopes of the Parthenon. In them we have the artist trying a subject over and over again in order to disengage an ideal, to get closer to some sort of quintessential expression. They do not always succeed; some, those perhaps in which there is not the authentic touch of Pheidias, are failures; but even in these the attempt was the same.

This also is the art of Sophocles: fine to the verge of thinness, precise to the verge of hardness; inimitable, impeccable, unpopular. It does not appeal to sentiment. In the ordinary mind it rouses admiration rather than enthusiasm. Even among trained critics the admiration is reluctant and qualified. "There are few people," it has been recently said, I know not with what truth, "who make Sophocles their favourite." But this is not all. Professor Murray finds in him "a bluntness of moral imagination," and "a conventional idealism." "Sophocles is the one Greek writer," he says elsewhere, "who is classical in the vulgar sense."

Statements like this give one pause. Clearly there

must be some sort of basis for them, or they could not be made by responsible authorities. But what is their basis? what do they mean? They mean this at least, though this does not exhaust their significance: that Athenian art, like the whole Athenian life of which it was the pattern and expression, creates a reaction. The Athenian empire in poetry, as in politics, had the effect of exciting, in those who lived with it or under it, a strange mixture of fascination and hatred.

All we have wandered from thy ways, have hidden
  Eyes from thy glory and ears from calls they heard;
Called of thy trumpets vainly, called and chidden,
  Scourged of thy speech and wounded of thy word.

We have known thee and have not known thee; stood beside
    thee,
  Felt thy lips breathe, set foot where thy feet trod,
Loved and renounced and worshipped and denied thee,
  As though thou wert but as another God.

All great art creates this reaction sooner or later. The attempt to include life, to express it wholly and essentially, becomes an attempt to limit life; and life will not be limited. This is the ultimate failure of all ideals, in art as in politics. They try to fix something which moves, which lives by moving. The progress of life bursts them, or moves away from them and leaves them empty. Even if there be such a thing as perfection—and the Athenian genius aimed at nothing less than perfection—there is no finality. But such an art sets a mark for all future art. Poetry has for all time to be judged, one might say, by an Athenian standard, as life itself has to be judged by

Athenian ideals. This is the gift which Athens has given, the task which Athens has set, to the world.

Let us try then to consider Sophocles as a poet, and to indicate the quality of his poetry. This, like the quality of the Athenian genius itself, almost eludes definition. In writing about Sophocles, critics are perpetually evading the point, or it might be more accurate to say that the point is perpetually evading them. They slide off into discussions of his verbal technique, the remarkable way in which he brings the vocabulary and structure of his poetry close alongside of prose; or of his stage-craft, the adroit mechanism of his drama; or still oftener, of his ethics and theology. But these are not his poetry; and it is by no means easy to keep the eye steady on the poetry.

The life of Sophocles (495 to 406 B.C.) just fills the century of the ascendancy of Athens. He outlived Aeschylus by fifty years. As a boy he led a chorus after Salamis; he died in extreme old age, a few months after Euripides, and just before the final collapse of Athens. His production, like that of Tennyson, extends over more than sixty years, and up to the end it was of unimpaired suavity and power. He retained beyond the age of Michael Angelo the accomplishment of Raffaele.

The seven plays we possess all belong to the latter part of his life. The *Antigone* is not later than 441 B.C.; the *Philoctetes* was produced in 409; the *Oedipus at Colonus*, presumably his last work, was only published some years after his death. The other four plays may be placed with reasonable certainty between the *Anti-*

gone and the *Philoctetes.* Over all the seven plays there is little poetical difference, little change of style and method. The vocabulary is substantially the same; so is the versification. His work shares the general extension of dramatic method which was going on throughout his life, and of which he is named as in certain definite matters one of the innovators or pioneers. In the two latest plays there is a more complex or episodic dramatic treatment. There is also a new metrical treatment of the lyrics, attributable, it would seem, to some contemporary change in the art of music. The chorus in the *Philoctetes* is on its way to becoming an atrophied organ in the structure of the drama, and is almost negligible. But these and similar points, though interesting, are superficial; they hardly touch the quality of his work as poetry: and that quality is in its main essence uniform. This is so, whether we regard it primarily on its formal side as art, or with regard to the interpretation and embodiment of life which it conveys.

The poetry of Sophocles on its formal side is most easily though not most accurately described by negatives. It has not salient points; a poetical manner has seldom if ever been so free from anything that can be called mannerism. It is like that of Horace in what we might almost describe as an impersonal or abstract quality. It does not depend for its effects on massed light and shade. It has little of the chromatic quality which is needed to stir the more sluggish or more worn senses. It does not deal in mystery as a background or contrast; its mystery is in its own essence and texture. Ornament in it is reduced to the lowest dimensions; for the lines and planes of the composition are the ornament. In all the seven plays there are only some half-dozen formal similes; and even these are brief, subdued, not enriched and heightened for their own sake. Language produces its effects by reserve. One of the rare instances in which Sophocles has allowed himself to embroider and enrich language for its own sake is worth citing, to show what an immense and masterful reserve his was, and what an effect he can produce by the least deflection from it, the least concession to romantic or ornamental treatment. "In this cool, pearl-grey, quiet place," as Pater says of the Ansidei Raffaele, "colour tells for double." The passage I mean is in the famous ode on Athens, the first stasimon in the *Oedipus at Colonus*. The first ten lines of this ode are perhaps the best known, the most popular passage in the whole of Sophocles. The love of his own birthplace, the just perceptible relaxation of treatment which is noticeable in this latest of his plays, a touch of romance that seems to enter and suffuse the almost colourless transparency of his style, combine to make the passage remarkable, and to distinguish it from the ordinary Sophoclean manner. Yet even here how sparing is the colour, how light and pure the ornament! The passage is suggested by, and bears distinct reference to, the equally famous passage in the nineteenth book of the Odyssey, which I have already cited as the crucial instance of epic passing beyond itself, reaching outwards to become lyric. From that passage of rich, crowded, intricate and delicate ornament Sophocles has taken two or three phrases, as if to emphasise and acknowledge the relation, and reset them "like stones of worth that thinly placèd are" in his own ode. It is a notable instance of his pre-eminent sense of language, a sense that makes him deal with language as a thing too precious to waste. Just this keen, exquisite sense of language, of the potency and inexhaustible significance of the word, is always present with him. In the *Oedipus at Colonus* the power of the word—"the little word," σμικρὸς λόγος—is a recurrent note. Language, to one who had been working in it with exquisite truth and delicacy for half a century, has become something awful. Oedipus traces his exile and misery to a little word. A little word pledges Theseus and the whole power of Athens. In the most splendid speech of the play, that of Oedipus on the triumph of Time, the little word once more is the power which shatters alliances and brings kingdoms to ruin.

This speech of Oedipus (ll. 607–620) is one of those passages in Sophocles which can be best commented on by saying that they are characteristically and essentially Shakespearian. There is no third writer, I think, who has ever written in just this manner. One can hardly speak of their style; they are beyond style. Language in them has become transfigured. One hardly notices the words; they have become translucent; it seems as if the poet who could do these things with these words could do anything with any words. Such power over language, or such insight into language, only comes once in the history of any single race. Many of the single lines and phrases in Sophocles have this intense and poignant quality. They do not come much in set speeches; they are not led up to; no special stress is laid on them. They just happen; and each time what happens is a miracle. In the

πάτερ, πιθοῦ μοι, κεἰ νέα παραινέσω

of Antigone; or in the

ὡς ὧδε τοῦδ' ἔχοντος αἰάζειν πάρα

of Tecmessa; or in the words of Hyllus,

μεταίτιος σοί τ' αὖθις ὡς ἔχεις ἔχειν,

the language is so simple, so apparently unconscious and artless, that its overwhelming effect makes one gasp: it is like hearing human language uttered, and raised to a new and incredible power, by the lips of some one more than human. It is the speech of one who may speak softly, and need not raise his voice to make it heard clear through any storm of sound. It is so in Shakespeare likewise; in the strangely thrilling phrases of simple words in simple order, but reaching without effort the highest heights of poetry. There is this note, common to Sophocles and Shakespeare, and beyond them perhaps unknown, unless it may be shared by Dante, in Macduff's

I cannot but remember such things were;

or in Edgar's

Men must endure
Their going hence, even as their coming hither;

or in Imogen's

I hope I dream.

Thus, too, not only the phrases but the single words in Sophocles have to be gazed into, pored over, held long in solution, before they will yield their full meaning. The whole problem and lesson of the *Antigone* may be said to lie in the conflict, only stated or hinted in the variation of a single term, between the ἀβουλία of Antigone and the δυσβουλία of Creon; the difference has not been more finely or more completely put by all that his expounders have embroidered upon it. In that same play the tragic view of the part played by love in human life is embodied in a single epithet, "light-minded," ἀπάτα κουφονόων ἐρώτων—repeated, at an interval of nearly three hundred lines, from the majestic Ode on Man, where it is said of him that among his marvellous achievements, κουφονόων φῦλον ὀρνίθων ἀμφιβαλὼν ἄγει καὶ θηρῶν ἀγρίων ἔθνη. For the full appreciation of what is implied one should also bear in mind the reference to love as an ἄγριος δεσπότης in the saying of Sophocles quoted by Plato in the opening scene of the *Republic*. These are only a couple of instances taken at random out of hundreds.

With this exquisite sense of the power and strangeness of language is connected another feature in the art of Sophocles, that of using the same words to mean many different things. He always deals with language as something complex and organic, like life; the "little word" has many meanings. It means different things in the mouth of each one who uses it, and to the apprehension of each one who hears it. It is no mere token passed from hand to hand, but a live element, almost itself a person. This is what lies at the foundation of the celebrated Sophoclean irony. The word spoken is more than the expression of the speaker's meaning. He made it, but once made, it is a living thing, carrying in it, it may be, the issues of life and death. This so-called irony in Sophocles is unfathomable. One of the most wonderful instances of it is in the scene of the *Electra* where Clytemnestra and Electra have just heard from the Paidagogos the account of the death of Orestes: a scene remarkable among other things for making Clytemnestra use more than one phrase which is almost verbally repeated by Shakespeare's Macbeth. Not a word that any one of the three says but means something different to the speaker, to each of the two hearers, and to us. For dramatic complexity and compression this scene is all but unequalled. One feels as though in an electric storm, played about by a hundred lightnings. And it is all done without what is called action, by the yet more potent and yet more living energy of the word.

Or take another instance of a different kind, going beyond the scope of what is ordinarily called tragic irony, as it also goes beyond the bounds of a single drama. There is no more striking instance of the sense in Sophocles of language as something which is alive and always re-embodying itself than the speech of the guard to Creon in the *Antigone*,[1] the one beginning

ἄναξ, βροτοῖσιν οὐδέν ἐστ' ἀπώμοτον.

The earlier scene between the two is one of the rare incursions made by Sophocles into the sphere of

[1] l. 388 foll.

comedy. The ponderous, Dogberry-like wit with which the guard began had dropped, when he became thoroughly frightened, into a vernacular babble. Here he reappears, quit of his terror and in high spirits; and his reflections now are a travesty, so true to life that it makes one feel sick, of the great speech of Aias—

ἅπανθ' ὁ μακρὸς κἀναρίθμητος χρόνος
φύει τ' ἄδηλα καὶ φανέντα κρύπτεται,
κοὐκ ἔστ' ἄελπτον οὐδέν, ἀλλ' ἁλίσκεται
χὠ δεινὸς ὅρκος καὶ περισκελεῖς φρένες.

All strangest things the multitudinous years
Bring forth, and shadow from us all we know.
Falter alike great oath and steeled resolve,
And none shall say of aught 'This may not be.'[1]

These are but brief suggestions of what might be indefinitely expanded. Let us pass now to the other side of poetry, and look, even more summarily, on the poetry of Sophocles as an embodiment and interpretation of life. It is here that we must weigh and must, I think, wholly dissent from the phrases "conventional idealism" and "bluntness of moral imagination."

The envisagement of life which underlies the Sophoclean drama is given most sharply in the morals—so we may call them, though the word must not be taken in too narrow a meaning—which Sophocles himself has attached to or incorporated in five out of the seven plays. The final note in *Oedipus the King* is "Human life, even in its utmost strength and

[1] *Aias*, 646 foll. The translation is Calverley's.

splendour, hangs on the edge of an abyss." In the *Oedipus at Colonus* it is "Let lamentation be brief, for what has happened was ordained." In the *Antigone* it is "Lack of wisdom ('unrede,' ἀβουλία) is the greatest of evils." In the *Aias* it goes still deeper; it is the necessity of tragedy for the purpose of life; men must see, must have actual experience, in order to know. Finally, in the *Trachinians* it takes shape in what is the ultimate and central message of Sophocles, his last word on life, "Look, and wonder, and think."

The endless wonderfulness of life—its splendour and fascination and unfathomable depth of meaning; this is what Sophocles gives us. It is neither ethics nor theology; it is something which, if we can but realise it, is larger and deeper. Creeds change; systems pass; this remains. "Those," says Shelley in the *Defence of Poetry*, "in whom the poetical faculty, though great, is less intense, as Euripides, have frequently affected a moral aim, and the effect of their poetry is diminished in exact proportion." Aeschylus had justified the ways of God to man, and vindicated law. Euripides, finding neither God nor law, but only burning instincts on the one hand and destructive thought on the other, launches out into a restless search that has no starting-point and no goal. Sophocles does not affect to explain life; he hardly criticises it. He shows things happening and how they happen, but not why. If he accepts conventions, it is because they are actual facts; they exist, and are among the motive forces of the world. If he seems to lack moral imagination, it is because morality is not with him a separate thing, with boundaries at which imagination can stop. Morals and religion are to him neither the foundations nor the superstructure; they are elements or functions of the one amazing and incomprehensible thing, the one thing that matters, the one thing that is,—life.

The clarity of the thought in Sophocles masks its profundity, just as the clarity of his language masks its poetic quality. We have to look long and steadily at both before they will yield their secret. Those pellucid depths seem shallow to the careless observer; that language, so exquisite and seemingly so effortless, produces at first sight the impression of being almost prosaic. He never seems to have any difficulty in saying what he means. But even to an Athenian audience, with their quick, trained intelligence, much of his meaning must have been lost. He knew this, and wrote accordingly. This is the final touch of the Sophoclean irony. The few anecdotes of him which have been preserved, his few criticisms on his own work and that of others, reinforce this impression; in all of them he says the exact truth very simply, and as though he did not take much pains to explain or argue, and did not concern himself much whether he was understood or not. It is the accent of one thinking aloud, seeing clearly and saying exactly what he sees, but not interpreting or commenting upon it. This accent is remarkable, for instance, in the words of his, already cited, at the beginning of Plato's *Republic*, or in his reply to Peisander quoted by Aristotle,[1]

[1] *Rhetoric*, iii. 18.

giving his reason for assenting to the oligarchic revolution of 411 B.C. It is pre-eminently so with the most famous of his sayings, that quoted by Aristotle in the *Poetics*: "I make persons as they should be made, Euripides makes them as they are." Even Aristotle misses, at least he does not bring out, the full significance of this profound and many-facetted sentence. What he meant—if one may infer his meaning from study of his actual productions—was not that his persons were conventionally idealised; it was that they were more real than reality. His characters express themselves often, we may think, inadequately: quite so; that is because he creates and envisages them vitally, and it is they who speak and act, as though with an independent substantive life of their own. Thus it is that on the one hand what they say is often so close to the vocabulary and structure of everyday Attic speech, that it is best illustrated from, and has to be studied by scholars in connection with, the idiom and language of contemporary prose authors. Thus, too, it is that on the other hand it often seems to fall short of the occasion, and has given rise to the charge that the people of Sophocles are stiff and conventional. They do not, like those of Aeschylus, speak a superhuman language, as

> When a God gives sign
> With hushing finger, how he means to load
> His tongue with the full weight of utterless thought,
> With thunder and with music and with pomp.

They do not, like those of Euripides, express themselves fully in that liquid and flexible speech which is the voice of Euripides and not theirs, which follows out the intricacies of thought and feeling with the skill of an analyst and the copiousness of a trained rhetorician. What they say is often a mere hint of what they think and feel. The speech of Tecmessa over the dead body of Aias[1] is a case in point. She says little, and what she says is in a low tone: but it is just what a woman would say. Euripides would make her say all that he knew she felt. But if she could say what she felt, she would not be Tecmessa. The tragic irony in Sophocles lies in the very fact that she can express so little of what she feels; his unique poetical genius lies in his power of making us realise her in and through her very inexpressiveness. Dryden says finely of Virgil that he had the gift of expressing much in little and sometimes in silence. That is equally true, though in a different way, of Sophocles. One may apply to his work—also with a difference, for every great artist is himself and unique—what Mr. W. P. Ker says, with his characteristic insight and precision, of the Icelandic work of the best period: "It belongs to a small class of fine literature, which begins in imagination and dramatic sense, and has been trained to use its imagination sincerely. It is neither 'classical' nor 'romantic,' though it is often both. It is simply right."

They are "simply right"—*οἵους δεῖ*—this is what one has to come back to, over and over again, with the characters of Sophocles. They are not abstract types. He does not use them as the mouthpieces for the

[1] *Aias*, 961–73.

expression of his own thoughts, or views, or speculations. Nor are they copies from actual people—*οἷοί εἰσιν*. Like the finest Greek sculpture, they move within the sphere of a strict convention; but within and through that convention they go to the centre; they do the utmost of what art can do with life.

Whenever we feel inclined to say that Sophocles is conventional or inadequate or superficial we ought to make sure that the fault is not with us—that it does not lie in the superficiality of our own view, the inadequacy of our own appreciation, some facile unconventionality of our own which is only a new kind of convention. Even what are called his false notes may often yield to more careful study a depth of insight which we had not suspected, and throw fresh light on the whole meaning of the scene or the play in which they occur. Let me give one instance. The Deianeira of the *Trachinians* is by common consent one of the most exquisite creations of poetry. For tenderness, delicacy, unselfishness, she stands alone in the classic, almost alone even in the romantic drama. She has been called, not unjustly, the Imogen among the women of antiquity. There must be few readers of the *Trachinians* who have not been disturbed, almost shocked, by what seems one false note put into her mouth by Sophocles. When she has explained to the Chorus her device for recovering the love of Heracles, she begs them to keep it hidden: "For in the dark," she says, "even if one does what is shameful, one will not fall into shame."[1] It sounds unlike

[1] *Trach.* 597.

her; it sounds a sophistry, some *cliché* of the rhetoricians such as inferior dramatists are fond of using. It is really the keynote to the whole tragedy; indicated, according to the wont of Sophocles, so lightly and subtly as to be almost invisible unless we bring to it our most sensitive and most perfectly trained intelligence. "It would be a waste of words," Professor Campbell says, in commenting on the play, "to enlarge upon the pathos of her fate." Yes; but her fate would be less pathetic than horrible, it would be a piece of meaningless and purposeless cruelty, were it not for this single momentary light flashed upon the inner reality of the situation. For she also, like Desdemona rather than like Imogen, broke the law, and was broken by it. There is another famous parallel in our own literature. Richardson's Clarissa was regarded, by the whole generation whom she melted and maddened, as an innocent and faultless creature dragged to ruin by incarnate powers of wickedness. Mrs. Thrale has recorded for us the searching and illuminating criticism of Richardson's greatest admirer. "When I mentioned Clarissa," she writes in her *Anecdotes of Dr. Johnson*, "as a perfect character, 'On the contrary,' said he, 'you may observe that there is always something which she prefers to truth.'"

Thus too in the *Antigone*, Ismene, the most fully and pathetically human of all the characters, is so lightly and subtly drawn, that she hardly yields her meaning to an eye that is not fixed on her, that does not dwell on her long enough or carefully enough to realise that she gives the central human note in relation to which all the other characters group themselves. The play has that quality of bitterness—that harsh or austere flavour—which Sophocles is said to have noted as a feature of his own art in its middle period. Of Antigone herself, the description of the Chorus," savage child of a savage father"—γέννημ' ὠμὸν ἐξ ὠμοῦ πατρός—is exactly true. The tone of the play is like that of a *King Lear* in which Lear is dead and the Cordelia of the first act is the central figure. It may be noted, too, that just as in *King Lear* an added touch of savagery is given by the implied motherlessness of the king's daughters, so in the *Antigone* there is hardly a reference to Iocasta. Antigone calls her brother τὸν ἐξ ἐμῆς μητρός (l. 467), and ὅμαιμος ἐκ μιᾶς (l. 513). These phrases hardly count. The only other mention of her mother is in her great dying speech and confession—

> κάρτ' ἐν ἐλπίσιν τρέφω
> φίλη μὲν ἥξειν πατρί, προσφιλὴς δὲ σοί,
> μῆτερ.

That single delicate, piercing touch is all.

Antigone, a Cordelia with the added gift of copious and powerful speech—it is Ismene whose voice is ever low and brief—is the direct antithesis to Deianeira. Her hard inflexible truthfulness is free, like Cordelia's, from selfishness, or at least from any but an intellectual self-regard, but it is without indulgence and without pity. The atmosphere of the play is given at the first stroke in the opening scene, under the hard, shadowless light of dawn in the silent palace-courtyard. The slight girlish figure of Ismene gives the normal human plane against which the others stand out like people of iron. In her we can measure them on the scale of common human weakness, of common human sympathy and generosity and emotion. After Antigone has gone out alone to certain death, Ismene is seen in the palace, mad with grief and terror. When sent for, she arrives with her face flushed and swollen, still in a passion of tears. She is loving, helpless, almost inarticulate, until, at a line of deliberate insult flung at Antigone by Creon, she breaks out into one great cry of love and indignation, and then disappears out of the action that goes rushing on to its doom.

I have mentioned the *mise-en-scène* at the opening of the *Antigone*. It is, as is usual with Sophocles, very lightly indicated by a few touches. Athenian art almost dispensed with background. There is one striking exception to this general rule in the famous opening of the *Electra*, where the rising sunlight has chased night and her stars away, and the lovely land with her cities rings to the morning voices of birds. Landscape and atmosphere are still more strongly marked in the *Trachinians*, and this is one of the features which give that play a distinctly romantic note. All through it the air is close and breathless. The town and its cattle-meadows lie in a cup of the hills, with the unshorn hill-pastures high above, and higher yet, thunder muttering and darkness gathering about the forests of Mount Oeta. The close air, the half-empty masterless palace, the hum and murmur of the excited town below, accentuate a sense of menace and misfortune that has already made itself felt in the opening words of Deianeira. These opening words are, in their place, unique. They almost repeat the closing words, the moral, of the *Oedipus the King;* it is as though Sophocles meant to indicate by a single strange touch, that the thing that hath been is the thing that shall be; that the old story of unhappiness—λόγος ἀρχαῖος ἀνθρώπων—renews itself among mankind, and that life itself is tragedy. The close, thunderous air of Trachis is, by another touch of subtle art, put in contrast with Iole's own country—διήνεμος πάτρα—the fresh, windy land that seems now so near and now so far off.

This sense of background helps to give the *Trachinians* its unmistakeable accent of romance. In the *Philoctetes* the romantic note is stronger, but it is struck in a quite different way. The *Philoctetes* is a romance in something of the same sense in which the term is applied to the latest plays of Shakespeare, the *Winter's Tale*, the *Tempest*, *Cymbeline*. Like them, it unrolls a story rather than sets and solves a problem: it deals with a sort of life that actually happens. As in *Cymbeline*, a piece of supernatural machinery is carelessly and rather needlessly introduced at the end to bring the story to a conclusion. As in the *Tempest*, the scene lies on an uninhabited island, with the same inconsistency about its being ten leagues beyond man's life and yet upon a main highway of commerce and traffic. "You will see the spring, if it is there still," says Odysseus, as though the natural features of the island might themselves have changed since a ship last touched at it; yet it was from this very island that merchants and pedlars brought supplies to the camp before Troy. Still more remarkable is the way in which the play deals with what happened at Troy after the Iliad, that tract of romantic history which reappears in late Greek poetry, and which, later still, enthralled the imagination of the Middle Ages. "Hector is dead, and Troilus is dead." Nestor is a broken man since the death of Antilochus. Aias is gone; Achilles is gone; Patroclus is gone. Odysseus the bastard ("the servant of God," he calls himself) and his *âme damnée* Diomede fill the place of greater men. Thersites (as in Shakespeare's *Troilus and Cressida*) lives. "He would"—ἔμελλε—says Philoctetes; "no base thing ever yet perished; the Gods guard such well; they take a strange pleasure in turning wickedness and malignity back from the grave, and ever send righteousness and goodness thither. What can one make of this? how commend it? for while I praise God's providence I find God is evil."[1] Euripides himself never struck harder than this, or more daringly. Even from this, in his large, steady regard of life, Sophocles will not shrink; for this also is part of the miracle of life, that it is hung over an abyss of blackness, and that if the thin crust gives way below them, men go mad.

Sophocles seems to take advantage in this play of the freer handling possible in romance to do things

[1] *Phil.* 446–52.

he never does elsewhere. The drama is not only a romance but an enigma. It moves from mystification to mystification. As the lights shift, the figures seem to change their identity. One might almost fancy that the disguised merchantman reappears at the end freshly disguised as Heracles. Neoptolemus sometimes seems the dupe of Odysseus, the Roderigo to his Iago: sometimes he seems his confederate from first to last. What is the meaning of his revolt, or seeming revolt, at the end, when he defies Odysseus and offers to sail home with Philoctetes? He has no ship. Has Odysseus told him, what he did not tell him earlier in the play, that Troy not only cannot be taken without the arrows of Philoctetes, but cannot be taken without Philoctetes himself? Ourselves we only know this from what Heracles says at the very end. In any case, what Sophocles sets before us in this play is not merely the marvellousness, the awe and wonder, of life, but its baffling mobility and complexity.

Such at least is the effect produced upon one by the play. It may mean a mood in Sophocles; it may only mean that, to one who saw life steadily and whole, the dissolving effect of the romantic spirit, and the disillusion and blank negation in which romance ends under the overpowering touch of analysis, were also parts of the great miracle, neither more nor less wonderful than any other manifestation of life.

The *Oedipus at Colonus*, in detached scenes and passages more beautiful, more pathetic, more splendid than almost any other of the plays, belongs likewise to the class of romances in its loosely knit structure, its

*

digressions, a certain relaxation of the handling. Like the Shakespearian romances, it deals with things as they actually happen, but suffuses them with a strange glow of beauty. *Τί γὰρ τὸ μεῖζον ἢ κατ' ἄνθρωπον νοσεῖς*; says Theseus to Oedipus: even such woes as his belong to the daily human lot. To him, like Cleomenes to Leontes in the *Winter's Tale*, Sophocles seems to say—

> No fault could you make
> Which you have not redeem'd ; indeed, paid down
> More penitence than done trespass : at the last,
> Do as the heavens have done, forget your evil ;
> With them forgive yourself.

The signs which came to him—

> *σημεῖα δ' ἥξειν τῶνδέ μοι παρηγγύα,*
> *ἢ σεισμὸν ἢ βροντήν τιν' ἢ Διὸς σέλας·*
> *ἔγνωκα μέν νυν ὥς με τήνδε τὴν ὁδὸν*
> *οὐκ ἔσθ' ὅπως οὐ πιστὸν ἐξ ὑμῶν πτερὸν*
> *ἐξήγαγ' ἐς τόδ' ἄλσος—*

are like those which come to Posthumus in prison in the last act of *Cymbeline.* The strangely introduced passage on Egyptian habits of life (ll. 337 foll.) bears a curious resemblance to the equally irrelevant digression in Act II. of the *Tempest* where Gonzalo plans his ideal state: in both cases the lax construction of romance allows the dramatist to insert something that has nothing to do organically with the action or situation, but about which he had been reading and of which his head was still full. But the sense of the wonderfulness of life recedes in the *Oedipus at Colonus* before the sense of the omnipotence of time. The greatest speech in the play is not that relating to the disappearance of Oedipus; it is Oedipus' own speech to Theseus, the one which begins, "O dearest son of Aegeus, to the Gods alone belongs not old age nor death." And the deepest note of the play is struck when Theseus, a little earlier, declares that since he has "no power over the morrow" he will do justice and love mercy to-day.[1]

I have hardly touched so far on the central group of Sophoclean plays. The seven extant tragedies represent the considered selection of antiquity from the poet's whole work. But there was a still further selection, the μείων ἐκλογή, of three out of the seven: and we may have the more confidence in the judgment which selected the seven, because we can see for ourselves that the four classed by it in the second rank, splendid as they are, do not in fact attain unto the first three. Each of the three, the *Oedipus the King*, the *Aias*, and the *Electra*, would require a lecture, indeed a series of lectures, to itself. But each has a striking and unique quality of its own, of which it may be possible in a few words to give some hint or indication.

Oedipus the King is the culmination of the harder middle style of Sophocles. It represents, in that method, perfection. The astonishing skill of its construction has made it, since Aristotle, or even earlier—for Aristotle's tone implies an opinion already fixed and orthodox—the Sophoclean masterpiece, the typical Sophoclean play. It is hardly that. A masterpiece

[1] *Oed. Col.*, 607–628, 565.

it certainly is; but for once we may be inclined to think it over-weighted with technical accomplishment. The plot is of an almost mathematical perfection; it gives the same sort of intellectual excitement as one of those theorems in Newton's *Principia* which actually make the pulse go quicker as one follows them. The verse is polished like steel; the setting out, with its unusually large amount of single-line dialogue varied by long set speeches, retains a trace of archaic stiffness; the dramatic movement, as for instance in the first entrance of Creon, is also just a little hard. It shows throughout effortless mastery; but it has not quite to the degree we may find elsewhere the play of light and shade, the mellow harmony of tone, the suggestiveness and the appeal to imaginative emotion. It is placed justly at the head of Sophocles' work; it is not quite in the centre of his poetry.

The central heart of his poetry is found, I think, in the other two plays of the lesser selection. The *Aias* is unequalled for splendour and elevation, the *Electra* for brilliance and elasticity. Both have in the highest degree the quality for which the countrymen of Shakespeare have no better or higher name than Shakespearian. Aias himself, strangely unlike the Aias of tradition, the "beef-witted" lord of *Troilus and Cressida*, is the most eloquent of all dramatic heroes, and has the greatest range in his eloquence. Now (as in his moralising over the seasons) he is as fluent and fanciful as Richard II. Now, as in his invocation to the sun, he is like Othello in his last words for a sort of passionate dignity, whose language is absolutely simple where in any other dramatist's hands it would have been rhetorical. Now he rises to a lonelier height, to something of the loftiness of Shakespeare's Brutus, where after long debate with himself he at last sees death clear before him, and names for the conclusion of the whole matter one thing, *ἢ καλῶς ζῆν ἢ καλῶς τεθνηκέναι*, *virtù*, achievement, whether through life or through death.

Round the great central figure is grouped a whole portrait-gallery of princes: foremost among them Odysseus, with his cautious wisdom, redeemed from hardness by the touch of pity even for an enemy, as he reflects on the instability of life and the fragile tenure of fortune. "Seest thou," cries Athena to him exultingly, "how great is the strength of the Gods?" and his reply strikes the central keynote of tragedy, the pity and fear which are the lesson of mortal things.

> ἐποικτείρω δέ νιν
> δύστηνον ἔμπης, καίπερ ὄντα δυσμενῆ,
> οὐδὲν τὸ τούτου μᾶλλον ἢ τοὐμὸν σκοπῶν·
> ὁρῶ γὰρ ἡμᾶς οὐδὲν ὄντας ἄλλο πλὴν
> εἴδωλ' ὅσοιπερ ζῶμεν, ἢ κούφην σκιάν.[1]

In these sad and noble lines we seem to hear, more than elsewhere, Sophocles speaking in his own voice and giving final expression to his deepest thoughts in presence of the mystery and pain of life. On a second plane and grouped towards the end of the action are the other Achaean captains: Teucer, courageous,

[1] *Aias*, 121-6.

unimaginative, straightforward; Menelaus, with his Spartan combination of meanness and vindictiveness; and the remarkable figure of Agamemnon, the typical Greek dynast, hard and unsympathetic, yet with a certain intellectual force that raises him to a real elevation, when he declares that "the law must stand" —*κατάστασις γένοιτ' ἂν οὐδενὸς νόμου*—and that the living act idly in considering the dead; to whom Aias has simply ceased to exist or to matter—*ἀνδρὸς οὐκέτ' ὄντος ἀλλ' ἤδη σκιᾶς*—when the breath is out of his body. Against that group of grim men stands out the lovely portraiture of Tecmessa, wistful and gentle, with her simple eloquence and timid unheeded wisdom, the most appealing figure in the whole of ancient dramatic literature.

There remains the *Electra*. It is on the whole the most Sophoclean and the most Shakespearian of all the plays. Nowhere in Sophocles, nowhere perhaps in poetry, is there a greater sense conveyed of the victoriousness of life, of the way in which it rises anew over its own dead past, and lets old sins and sorrows fade away among forgotten things. As part of the miracle of life we are presented with the miracle of self-renewal.

The *Electra*, as the one instance in which we have a drama on the same subject by each of the three great Attic tragedians, gives in a rather unique way a test or gauge of the Sophoclean method. The *Libation-Carriers* of Aeschylus is not, to be sure, Aeschylus at quite his greatest; it is, comparatively speaking, in the slack water between the vast ocean-tide of the *Agamemnon* and the reflux of the *Eumenides*, "as the waves of the ebb drawing seaward when their hollows are full of the night." The *Electra* of Euripides, that masterly study in hysteria, is vitiated as poetry, like much of Euripides' work, by its subordination of creation to analysis. But between the two, the *Electra* of Sophocles has of late obtained, I will not say less than justice, but some failure of intelligent appreciation. It has been suggested that, if the play is not to be regarded as "a combination of matricide and good spirits," we must believe that Sophocles wrote it in reaction against the treatment of Euripides, and deliberately sought in it a "primitive" atmosphere and handling, returned deliberately upon an archaistic and unreal convention. It is true that we find in it—most notably in the dream of Clytemnestra and in the description of the chariot race—a remarkable reconstitution for dramatic purposes of the epic manner. But otherwise such criticism appears to miss both the fineness and the depth of Sophoclean art. Sophocles does not concern himself to justify, or to condemn, or even to explain; here as elsewhere he sets the wonder of life before us and lets us draw our own conclusions. This play has no words of summing up at the end, not even an awful and passionless line like that at the end of the *Trachinians*, "and naught herein but is of God." In the exit-speech of the Chorus he deliberately refrains from pointing any moral. It is tragedy carried beyond tragedy; it is art for the sake of life. Whether such a thing were possible in art we might doubt, were it not that the greatest artists have done it. Sophocles has done it here. If there is a fault to be found with the play, it is that Sophocles has carried in it his method of compression and reserve to a degree almost beyond the grasp of ordinary intelligence. The confession of Clytemnestra (l. 525 foll.) is as great as that made by her in the *Agamemnon*, but it is fined down into a needle-point. The single shriek of Electra when she hears the news of Orestes' death is a lightning-flash revealing for a moment gulfs of passion, and as suddenly withdrawn. Her other single line of self-revelation and self-condemnation (l. 1311), "the old hatred is molten into me," contains implicitly the self-torturing hysterical Electra of Euripides; but it is left alone and not worked upon. The murder of Clytemnestra is not suggested, or apparently contemplated by her; it comes suddenly upon her in one overwhelming moment. "They do the deed," she whispers: it is the exact phrase of Macbeth; and for the rest of that scene she can only speak in brief gasps, in choking half-lines. There is little enough of good spirits here; little enough of any primitive atmosphere, except in the sense in which life itself is primitive, and art the express image of life.

And thus to the *Electra*, as to the whole marvel and mystery of life embodied in the poetry of Sophocles, there is no solution; for a solution would imply that there was something beyond life and greater than life. Or if we can speak of a solution, it is simply this, that life goes on, renews itself, moves triumphantly forward for ever; in a word, that life is. One might almost say that to his art ethics and religion, the problems set and solved or declared insoluble by the thinkers, do not matter. Before his clear profound vision, ordinary ethics, ordinary religion, the common tissue of actual human feelings and thoughts and deeds, open up depths as wonderful as any reached by the masters of constructive systems or of destructive analysis. This is the first and last message of Sophocles, if one can speak of the message of a supreme art. *Say not in thine heart, who shall ascend into heaven?* like Aeschylus, *or, who shall descend into the deep?* like Euripides: *the word is nigh thee, even in thy mouth and in thy heart.* With a power, an ease, a skill which are the culminating achievement of the Greek genius, he employs the endless miracle of language to express and interpret, to set out in clear faultless pattern, the fathomless miracle of life.

AFTER ATHENS

I

THE ALEXANDRIANS

In the fifth century before Christ, Greek poetry had concentrated at high tension in Athens. Throughout that century, the most thrilling, the most crowded, the most dramatic of all in human history, Athens was Greece in the field of letters no less than in that of thought and of politics. She held the empire of poetry and imposed it upon the whole Hellenic world. The school of Athens absorbed or attracted into itself the intellect and imagination of Greece. Athenian poetry fixed the model and set the limit for poetic accomplishment. The effort, in poetry as in political and civic life, was too great for human powers to maintain. Both empires fell within the century of their foundation and within a few months of one another. Euripides and Sophocles both died early in the year 406 B.C. In the autumn of the next year, the whole Athenian fleet was captured in the Hellespont, and the long agony of the Peloponnesian war came to an end.

The effect, in both cases, is that of the lights being turned down. Greek history, from the fall of Athens to the Macedonian conquest, is a dismal record of confused aims, lowered ideals, intermittent patchings up which hardly checked a steady process of decay. Greek poetry during the same period almost ceased to exist. The vital movement of intelligence and imagination passed into prose. That new vehicle of expression had at last been fully mastered, and was reaching the climax of its powers in the hands of the orators, the historians, the philosophers. In the sphere of poetry the epoch is one of disintegration and diffusion. There is no new poet of the first or even of the second rank, until, in a completely changed world, we reach the masters of the school of Alexandria. Quite apart from the conquests of prose, poetry had, for the time, done all it could. The poets of the fifth century had become the classics; and there followed a long period of enfeebled and dwindling classicism. Lyric and dramatic poetry shared in the common decay. Even on the stage the masterpieces of the older tragedians overshadowed and killed the inferior genius of their successors. The dithyramb became vulgarised. The art of narrative poetry, of the epic in its wide sense, had been lost. The growth and vogue of the New Comedy on the one hand, the development of the essay and dialogue on the other, absorbed the function of poetry as an interpretation of life. People were on the one hand preoccupied in the literary or critical study of the older writers, and on the other hand had their attention fully engrossed with the profuse supply of miscellaneous work, most of it ephemeral and trivial, produced to meet the demand of a largely increased reading public.

The lights did not go out all at once, but those

that remained were few and faint. Aristophanes survived his two colleagues by about twenty years; but after the production of the *Frogs* he ceased, as it would seem, to be a lyric poet, while even his comedy, missing, as we may suspect, the inspiration of the great tragedy from which it was the reaction, and to which it was the complement, falls off in brilliance and imagination. Agathon, that interesting but rather elusive figure, in whose hands it had seemed that dramatic poetry might take a new range and a new lease of life, had disappeared into Macedonia, *ἐς μακάρων εὐωχίαν*, and ceased to be a living influence. "A good poet, and his friends regret him," is the strange and perhaps slightly sardonic epitaph pronounced over his poetical extinction. The one hundred and forty tragedians of whom some notice or record is left were, so far as we can judge, a mass of mediocrities and nonentities. Poetical plays were turned out as from a factory; the art or trick of composing them was taught in schools or guarded as a trade secret in families. One Sicilian house produced tragedies through four successive generations. A nephew of Aeschylus bequeathed what he himself had taken up as an inherited profession to a grandson and two great-grandsons. Both a son and a grandson of Sophocles were tragedians. The playwrights, to use in its exact meaning a term which has unfortunately become rubbed down by usage, were one section, and only one among others, of the great theatrical industry; they became first the colleagues, and then the subordinates, of the actor-manager. On the other hand the chamber-drama, brought to a high pitch of finish by Theodectes in the latter half of the fourth century, hardly professed to be poetry at all. Like the New Comedy, of which it was only a variant form, it retained the tradition of being written in metre. But for rhetorical, argumentative, or even familiar dialogue, the iambic, besides being what the public were accustomed to, was a vehicle which long practice had made even more facile in handling than prose; and it is probable that the great bulk of the fourth-century tragedies were not meant to be taken as poetry in any higher sense.

The multiplication of books and of readers was also the index, as well as a contributory cause, of the dwindling impulse of production in all those kinds of poetry which are classed together under the name of the lyric. Already, in the fifth century, collections of the poems of the earlier lyrists were habitually made to be read or sung: the old wine was preferred to the new. The institution of the dithyrambic contests, at Athens and elsewhere, may be interpreted as an attempt to prop up a decaying art by a system of bounties. The Odeum was built and endowed by Pericles with this specific object. But in the performances held there, poetry was subordinate to music; and the large prizes offered to successful dithyrambists had little or no effect in arresting, if they did not rather precipitate, the decline of lyrical and choral poetry. After the death of Sophocles, the most important figure in poetry of the generation which followed was Timotheus of Miletus. He was, as has been already mentioned, the most popular poet of his age. But his popularity was corrupt in its origin and disastrous in its effects. Clever, showy, and florid, his poetry debased the standard of taste all over Greece. The citadel of Hellenic culture, won so hardly and built up by such immense effort, was crumbling away. The Heliconian springs were laid open, and their waters spread in a shallow flood, tepid and turbid, over an exhausted Hellas and a half-Hellenised outer world. Only in a few minor and, if one may use the word, provincial poets of the fourth century, do the pure Hellenic tradition, the authentic note and accent, remain unimpaired; and their work is confined, so far as any extant examples go, to the briefer flights and narrower limits of the epigram. The Anthology preserves specimens of the work of three poets contemporary with the reign of Alexander, which in their purity of line, their reticence, their exquisite modelling and phrasing, continue the high tradition of Simonides and the Athenian or pre-Athenian classics. Two of the three, Adaeus and Phaedimus, are not Greeks of Greece Proper, but Macedonians. In their work there is a freshness, a serious gravity, which comes to us like a touch of keen pure northern air. The dialectical and rhetorical movement of their time has left them untouched; they are natural primitives in an age of decadence and eclecticism. The third, the Arcadian poetess Anyte of Tegea, is more remarkable still. Alone among her contemporaries she possesses the grand style; this is what is meant by the curious phrase "a woman Homer," used of her by a later critic, himself of the Macedonian school, and a poet of no mean order, Antipater of Thessalonica.[1] Together with this, she has a deep and delicate feeling for nature such as is rare in Greek work. The twenty epigrams of hers which are extant are not only the best of that age, but among the best of any period: in their quiet beauty and simple grace they are fit to stand—and no higher praise could be given them—beside the work of Simonides.

That the last notes of Hellenic poetry in its full purity and authentic tone come from outlying lands or remote hill-fastnesses is something more than an accident. It is a symbol of what was happening to Hellenic life. For the whole movement of that life, and of poetry with it, had become one of decentralisation. That term may bear more than one meaning, but in all its meanings it applies here. Like all vital functions, poetry is subject to a periodic movement, a rhythmic contraction and dilatation. The diffused poetical life of the sixth century B.C. had flooded in upon Athens and concentrated there. Now it ebbed outwards. But the world into which it passed out was immensely enlarged, and had lost its responsiveness to the poetical instinct. Life was on a larger scale, but at a lower tension and feebler vitality. The city of the Violet Crown, the city which had given a new life to Homer, which had gathered up the lyric and created the drama, became politically an unim-

[1] Ἀνύτης στόμα, θῆλυν Ὅμηρον, *Anth. Pal.*, ix. 26.

portant provincial town, and intellectually the seat of a cosmopolitan university. Greece in its old sense ceased to exist: the Hellenic life was absorbed and diluted in the quasi-Hellenised world of the Graeco-Macedonian empires. Earlier epochs of expansion had only reinforced the central life of the mother-stock: migrations and colonisations had enriched and expanded Hellenism; but now the scale of things was too great. The centre of poetry was lost.

It was lost so completely that when the instinct for poetry reasserted itself—for it cannot be destroyed—it had to start afresh, laboriously and to a large extent ineffectually, to try to find it again, without well knowing where to look for it. Poetry seemed a thing done with, an art of the past. It had ceased to be a living function and interpretation of life. Those who felt within them still the instinct for imaginative creation did not quite know what they would be at. They had no new interpretation of life to offer. They were overshadowed by their own classics. The great poets reared a menacing and seemingly insurmountable barrier between them and poetry. Ἅλις πάντεσσιν Ὅμηρος—"Homer is enough for anybody"—the remarkable phrase used by Theocritus, expresses not only the cynical doctrine of the outer world, but the deep-seated belief of scholars and the despondent conclusion of poets.

Yet it was among the scholars that the reaction began. The whole history of earlier Alexandrianism, a steady laborious poetical movement which went on at full pressure for something like half a century, is the history of an attempt to bring poetry back into touch with life, to reinstate it as a living art. This statement of the case may at first sight appear paradoxical. The Alexandrians are dismissed in common surveys of Greek literature, as little more than pedants. They are called artificial poets, as though all poetry were not artificial, and the greatest poetry were not the poetry of most consummate artifice. Their poetic instinct, except in one or two cases, is denied. That their poetic production was mingled with pedantry is true; it is true also that in their inferior work the pedantry is more conspicuous than the poetry. But we must go deeper. If they did not care for poetry, why did they practise it so incessantly and with such pains and devotion? The reason is simply this: that the centre of poetry having become lost, they were trying their best to find it. In this attempt they did not fully succeed. But if they did not recover poetry they made a serious advance on the way towards its recovery. They ploughed the fallows, and prepared the field for new seed. The Latin genius entered into the field they had prepared. The Alexandrians were the interpreters of Hellas and the forerunners of Ausonia. In either way their effective value in the life of poetry can hardly be overestimated. They filled up with their bodies, one might almost say, the gap that might otherwise have become an impassable chasm. They kept the poetry of the past alive, and nursed the seeds of the poetry of the future. But for them, Greek poetry might have perished out of the world. But for them, Latin poetry might never have come to the birth. We are too much accustomed to think of the Alexandrian period as one wholly of decadence, of imitative classicism, of a poetry based on literature and out of touch with life. Out of touch with life it was, for it was thus that after the gap of the fourth century B.C. the Alexandrians found it; but what they, or the best of them, tried hard to do, was to bring it into touch with life again in a new way. To do this they had to re-train the art; they set themselves to school for this purpose, with a touching and very modern belief in the saving virtue of education. Many of them stopped short there, and remained through life only learners, art-students and not artists. They were engrossed in the drill and technique of their art, never getting beyond the stage of studies and exercises, and finally losing sight of the end in the means, and settling down, like students in an art-school who never become painters, to the endless and enfeebling study of poetical mechanism. Imitators they were, as all beginners must be; and the weight of their own classics lay so heavy upon them that few of them, and these with a hard struggle, passed beyond imitation or got free to create. But as regards the progress of poetry, what gives the age its meaning is not that it was an age of decadence: it is that it was an age of difficult and delayed germination. The seeds of new life were under the surface. Out of a silver age, like that of Latin poetry under the Empire, nothing comes; it only dwindles away slowly and dies. But out of Alexandrianism came, with the touch of a new life in a new language, Latin poetry.

Thus we see the Alexandrian poets doing two things. They were not only copying and studying, though they copied industriously and studied incessantly; they were also searching and experimenting, trying to find out new forms for poetry and to adapt these forms to new subjects, trying, in a word, to bring back poetry into touch with life. They practised in almost every method, in order to strike out some new method, such as would effect what poetry wanted. An altered world called insistently for new means of imaginative expression, for a new interpretation of its meaning. With the break-up of Hellas, with the diffusion and decentralisation of Hellenism, the ideals of life and thought had also changed. The technique of art in its old sense had been mastered and become common property. Science had been definitely organised. The study of the physical world had become an important part of culture, and the study of the past, on its two sides of history and archaeology, was established as part of science. Working on these two lines, the imaginative or poetical instinct developed on the one hand out of the study of the physical world a new feeling for nature; on the other hand, out of the study of history and archaeology a new feeling for the romance of the past. Widened sympathy brought with it increased sensibility; and to this increased sensibility is to be ascribed the rapid growth and immense development of sentiment. The growth of sentiment is most strikingly marked as regards the treatment of love. Amatory poetry, the treatment of the psychology of passion and sentiment, sprang rapidly into a leading branch of the art. The discovery was made that matter existed on this side of human life which not only was inexhaustible in its appeal to the senses and the imagination, but admitted of infinite variations in treatment. *Les nuances d'amour sont infinies:* that discovery, made then in its fulness for the first time, had, as it always has had whenever it has been re-made, profound results, always interesting, sometimes disastrous, but, both for good and for evil, creating a new sphere, and one might almost say a new function, for art.

It is in view of these considerations that Alexandrian poetry, otherwise so confusing in its intricacy and so largely meaningless in its purport, can be best classified and appreciated. When I say classified, I should perhaps rather use a word less suggestive of the arrangement of a museum. For poetry was not dead; it was struggling, at a low vitality, painfully and laboriously, towards fresh life. Its value for us as poetry exists only in so far as we can feel in it the working of that process, and thus can relate it organically to the larger life of poetry. Looking at it in this way we may be able to grasp the imaginative value, the poetical object and meaning, of the specific forms which it took. Of these there are five, or five which are important: the elegy, the idyl, the pastoral, the so-called didactic poem, and the romantic epic.

Of the definition of the elegy, in some ways the most important, as it was the most largely cultivated, of all these forms, there will be more to say presently.

The idyl I use in its original and proper meaning to express what may, on the analogy of the term cabinet-picture in the art of painting, be called a cabinet-poem; a small detachable work, highly finished, complete in itself, and not designed to take a definite place in any larger imaginative interpretation or pattern of life. The pastoral and the romantic epic do not for our immediate purpose require any closer definition, which may be deferred for a fuller discussion of the two poets who were their first masters, Theocritus and Apollonius. The term didactic poem is an unhappy and gravely misleading one, but so embodied in usage that it may be conveniently employed instead of inventing a new name, so long as we keep clear of the false implication which its literal meaning would convey.

In each of these forms the attempt made by the Alexandrians was to create a new artistic vehicle which should be capable of bringing back poetry into relation with life. In the elegy they were trying to get poetry into relation with the smaller specialised interests—some more intimate, others more derivative or artificial—of a life in which the full synthesis had been lost and was not then recoverable. In the idyl they were trying to get poetry into relation with the place in life, the effect on life, of a matured and self-centred art. They were setting before themselves, for the first time, the ideal of art for art's sake, in the sense of an art which sets its own problems and has no conscious object beyond the artistic satisfaction of solving them. In the pastoral they were trying to get poetry into relation with the new feeling for nature: a feeling which had arisen partly in reaction from the intense civic life of a past age, partly in weariness of civilisation, partly in a natural process of psychological development such as may be traced in all literatures. In the didactic poem they were trying to get poetry into relation with science, with systematised knowledge based on observation, record, experiment and classification: knowledge of the physical universe in its constitution and processes, and also of the constitution and processes of the human mind in its threefold energies of thought, production, and conduct, the division laid down once for all by Aristotle. Finally, in the romantic epic all these motives were in some degree combined, but in subordination to another. A movement was made beyond them, in a fresh direction, towards a new synthesis of poetry. This was the movement which was carried on and completed by the genius of Virgil, and which was the last gift of Greece through Rome to the Middle Ages and the new world.

Thus the Alexandrian age represents the decentralisation of poetry in two senses: not only in the sense that Hellenic culture had ceased to be Hellenic and had become cosmopolitan, that its life, and the life of the poetry in which it found its artistic embodiment and imaginative interpretation, was no longer concentrated at a single point, but also in the more important sense that poetry had lost its centre and ceased to deal with life as a whole. But it represents also the feeling after a new recovery, the stirrings towards a fresh movement of progress. Alexandrianism did three things. In the first place, it collected, preserved, and annotated the texts of the Greek poets. Secondly, it kept the poetical mechanism, the method and technique of poetry as a fine art, in working order. Thirdly, as I have attempted to indicate, it began to set poetry itself on the way towards new developments. In all three ways its service to the world was so great as to merit more acknowledgment than it generally receives. The scholarship and technique of the Alexandrians are of course admitted, as they are beyond question. But the pedantries of a past age seldom find favour in the eyes of an age engrossed with new pedantries of its own; and we are a little too apt, I think, to judge Alexandrian poetry in the lump and not discriminate carefully or delicately enough between that in it which is dead matter, and that in which the life of poetry, though dormant or at low pressure, is still there.

The term Alexandrian bears two senses, which it is necessary to distinguish. In its larger sense it is used to include the whole of the Greek or quasi-Greek literature—for it was Hellenistic rather than Hellenic—belonging to the period of the great monarchies founded by Alexander's marshals. From the death of Alexander at Babylon until the annexation of Syria by the Roman Republic "made an end of an old song" and swept away the dwindled remains of the once vast Seleucid empire, there are a little more than two hundred and fifty years. These two centuries and a half include a very large poetical literature, from Philetas and Asclepiades at their commencement, through the rich period of Theocritus, Callimachus, Euphorion, and Aratus to the younger generation of Apollonius Rhodius, Rhianus, and Antipater of Sidon, and so on until it ends with Meleager and Parthenius. This poetry was widely diffused over the Eastern Mediterranean, to some extent in Greece Proper and the islands, but more largely in outlying and only partially Hellenised areas; in Sicily, Macedonia, Asia Minor, Syro-Phoenicia, Egypt and Cyrene. It had no national centre. But under the reign of Ptolemy II. it drew together at Alexandria, and from that time forward the term Alexandrian may be used in its other and more restricted sense to cover the poetry written or published there. Alexandria had become the largest and wealthiest city in the Hellenistic world. Men of letters naturally congregated to it, partly from an instinct of confederation, partly from the advantages offered by its university and library, its organised publishing trade, and the munificent patronage extended to literature by the court. Other literary centres enjoyed similar advantages, but not to the same extent. Aratus found his way from his birthplace in Cilicia to the court of Antigonus at Pella, where the Macedonian school of poetry was of some importance. Euphorion became chief librarian to Antiochus the Great. Poets gathered later round the Attalid court at Pergamum and the magnificent library founded there by Eumenes II. The Sicilian school, which had an old tradition, continued to flourish at Syracuse. Athens and Rhodes, though they were specialising more and more on the study of philosophy and oratory, retained a remnant of their older traditions. But Alexandria was the main centre; and the Graeco-Egyptian school of poets transmitted from the reigns of the earlier Ptolemies an impulse which long outlasted the Ptolemaic kingdom. It continued through the Roman and into the Byzantine period. In Palladas at the end of the fourth century, in Julianus and Tryphiodorus in the fifth, in Nonnus as late as the sixth, we can see that school of Alexandria still continuing a desultory and feeble activity when Alexandria itself had sunk into ignoble decay, and when the Latin poets who had owed so much to Alexandrian influence had themselves become the ancient classics of a lost culture.

In the wider and more general sense in which we speak of Alexandrian as distinguished from Greek poetry, Theocritus marks the point of transition. Of him as of none among his contemporaries it may be said that he effectively put new life into poetry, that he is a poet in the highest sense, though not a poet of the first rank. He is the first of the romanticists; while at the same time, in virtue of a precision of handling and purity of line which are like those of his more strictly Hellenic predecessors, he is the last of the Greek classics. He stands a little apart from, and a little higher than, the Alexandrian school to which he technically belongs; not because his notion of poetry, his ideals and methods, were materially different from theirs, but because he brought to poetry a higher felicity, a finer poetical instinct, and a more incommunicable personal quality.

Of Theocritus, the last of the Greek classics, as of Apollonius, the leader of the romantic revolt in poetry, I shall speak later. In the meantime I wish to resume the consideration of what may be called the central movement of Alexandrianism. To trace this among a multitude of names and through a mass of miscellaneous poetry of which, with but few exceptions, we possess only inconsiderable fragments, is not easy. Perhaps the clearest view may be got by restricting our survey to the third century and to a few of the most important names. These are Aratus, Callimachus, and Euphorion. Among them, the three give the main central type.

Of Euphorion there is little to say, because nearly all his poetry has disappeared. He seems to be one of those poets who have, through some conjunction of circumstances to which the clue is now lost, exercised an influence quite disproportionate to their merit or accomplishment. Partly this is because they hit, more exactly than their contemporaries, the predominant taste of the generation succeeding their own. Partly it comes from those chances which label a school with the name of one rather than another of those who jointly founded or developed it. His effect on Roman taste at the critical period of the development of Latin poetry was decisive. His name became the symbol not only of a poetical school, but of a way of regarding poetry. On Virgil himself, in the early period when he was under the influence of Gallus, Euphorion must have had an effect that might have been disastrous on a less balanced or more precocious genius. The way in which he is coupled by Lucian with Parthenius, Virgil's own tutor, is one among many indications that Euphorionism was recognised as a specific poetical tendency which continued for at least two centuries, and which left its traces deeply marked upon the world. It appealed very powerfully to young poets, both by its unrestrained indulgence of sentiment and by its profuse ostentation of scholarship. But except with those few who had the strength of innate genius to outgrow it, it was a demoralising influence: and the ill deeds that men do live after them.

Aratus was, like Euphorion, the founder of an important school. He represents that side of the Alexandrian movement which sought to find a new centre for poetry in modern science. Organised science, the study of the physical universe, was the most important and most characteristic intellectual growth of the period. Building on the foundations laid by Aristotle, students devoted themselves in large numbers and with assiduous industry to investigating, cataloguing, and recording the facts of nature. But except in the field of pure and applied mathematics, the science of the Alexandrians dealt less with the discovery of laws and tracing out of natural processes than with the preliminary task of enumeration and classification. This is a task which, however important and necessary, is little fitted to kindle the imagination. Pre-Socratic science had dealt in large imaginative generalisations, and had produced poetry like that of Empedocles. At a later epoch, when natural science had dwindled again into something ancillary to an ethical interpretation of life, the physical doctrines of Epicurus became the basis for the majestic poetry of Lucretius. With Aratus and the Alexandrians it is different. They have no scientific imagination. Facts are noted chiefly for their own sake, and beyond this, either for their immediate practical utility or for their associations with mythology and literature. In the science of astronomy, indeed, there is something which has an inherent power over the imagination, through the mere vastness and mysteriousness of the objects with which it deals, and their overpowering contrast with the brief and transitory life of man. Astronomers no less than poets have felt that their science had in it something divine. This feeling has never been more briefly or nobly expressed than in the well-known epigram by the greatest of the ancient astronomers. "I know," says Ptolemy, "that I am a mortal and of a day, but when I scan the close-woven circling spirals of the stars, no longer do my feet touch earth, but I sit by God himself and take my fill of the immortal divine meat."[1] Nature can haunt the man of science also like a passion, and make him for a moment into a poet; and here, even in the decayed world of the Antonines, imagination could kindle into expression, and a flower of poetry rise out of the dusty withered Alexandrian stem.

Of all this there is little in Aratus, and still less in Nicander and the rest, who are classed together as belonging to his school. The imaginative aspect of science does not tell in his work; and this is

[1] *Anth. Pal.*, ix. 577.

because he was not himself a trained investigator of nature, but a man of letters who was interested in science from the outside. The consequence is that in him there is a gap left between science and life. His poetry is not organic. In the matter of the *Phaenomena* he versifies Eudoxus, in that of the *Diosemeia* he versifies Aristotle and Theophrastus. He felt, as his whole age felt, that in Empedocles they found something which they did not find in Homer; but they did not realise clearly that what was essential and common in both Empedocles and Homer was a vision, an imaginative interpretation of life. Early science had been inarticulate poetry; the later articulate science could not be made back into poetry except by an imaginative effort of which the poets of that time were incapable.

The extraordinary and long-continuing popularity of the *Phaenomena* and *Diosemeia* has long been one of the puzzles of literary criticism. It was universal in the Hellenistic world; it was equally great at Rome. In Cicero's translation not less than in the original they had a profound influence over the development of the poetical art of Virgil. They were a model, and more than a model, we may say deliberately a source of inspiration, to the later Augustans like Ovid and Manilius. In the next generation Germanicus translated them anew, and they were still being re-studied and re-translated as late as the end of the fourth century, in that last impulse of neo-Alexandrianism which preceded the Dark Ages. The clue to that extraordinary influence and popularity is perhaps to be found where one would not at first think of looking for it. Quintilian, summing up in brief chosen words the trained judgment of Latin criticism, dismisses Aratus' poetry in a single depreciating sentence. *Motu caret,* he says of it, *ut in qua nulla varietas, nullus adfectus, nulla persona, nulla cuiusquam sit oratio.* It was just this stillness and motionlessness, this absence of play, of sentiment, of impersonation, of rhetoric, that gave the work of Aratus its singular effect and fascination. Sentiment and rhetoric and impersonation were the stock-in-trade of later Greek literature, and continued to be so through the rest of the classical and sub-classical period. But in fact the world was more than half sick of them, though it could not keep its hands off them, and kept returning to them again and again, with a sort of involuntary fascination. In the poetry of Aratus it felt that it had got down to something solid and wholesome, poetry in its lowest terms perhaps, but poetry that had got its feet clear of restlessness, sentimentalism, and unreality. The mythological episodes in the *Phaenomena,* it has been noticed, are few and brief. There is high polish, but little ornament. Aratus may be pedantic, but he is not meretricious. The work is all in studiously low tones. In a period of forced and fatiguing chromatic harmonies, he works almost in monochrome. In a period of exaggerated sensibility, he is dry and hard. This lowness of tone suffices in the careless ordinary judgment for dismissing him as no poet, because devoid of poetical imagination. It is difficult to be sure how far it is in fact due to want of imagination, and how far to severity of method; whether it is the absence of sensibility or the reaction against it. In his search after something in poetry that should not be mere ornamental trifling, he discards not merely the egoism of passion, the lax demoralising treatment of life characteristic of the school of Euphorion, but the human element in nature.

To produce poetry under these conditions is difficult; but the difficulty of the task, as Lucretius said later of his own poem, was part of its charm. Only, there is this difference, and it is vital: that in Lucretius the poet's own extraordinary personality kindles his whole work, while in the poetry of science as the Alexandrians conceived it, personality has to be suppressed and eliminated. This was with them, very largely at least, a reaction against the dominance of Euripides. The effect of Euripides on Greek poetry after him, though it is now fully realised, has perhaps never yet been fully worked out, particularly as regards the movement of recoil which necessarily follows the first effect of any great influence, and which combines with the persistence of that influence to create conditions of intricate complexity. At all events, the work of Aratus and of the school which he represents gave a stiffening to poetry which is of great moment in its history. The term stiffening may be used in two senses, good and bad, and both senses apply here. But if we look to the end—if we look to Virgil, for the sake of whom, one would like to say, if one could say it without being misunderstood, the whole Alexandrian school existed—the influence of Aratus is not one of the least important of those which went to create the marvel of the Georgics.

The schools of poetry represented by Euphorion and Aratus are two sides, partly antagonistic and partly complementary, of the attempt to find a new embodiment for the decentralised and disintegrated life of poetry. But neither of them is the main Alexandrian movement, the movement which was central so far as we can use such a term at all of a period when the centre had been lost. That movement is more closely connected with the name of Callimachus. It had begun to take shape a generation earlier, before the school of Alexandria had been fully formed. Its beginnings were in an Ionian school which inherited a fragment of the intellectual empire of Athens. The two originators of it were the Colophonian Antimachus and the Coan Philetas.

Too little of the work of these poets survives to enable us to form any full judgment of its quality. Antimachus was the founder of the new elegy, in which the Ionian genius returned, with a difference, to its earlier path in the pre-Athenian period of Greece. His pupil and countryman Hermesianax continued his work. Professor Murray has made a fertile suggestion, which I hope will not be allowed by him to drop, that the long fragment of this poet preserved in Athenaeus might be taken as a starting-point for the investigation and elucidation of Alexandrianism as a matter of literary history. For the study of Philetas even such material as this fails: we may guess him to have been both a finer poet and a more interesting personality than Antimachus; but in the total loss of his works we know little more of him than that he was the poetical master not only of Callimachus, but of Theocritus. It was by Antimachus and Philetas that poetry was rescued, so far as it was rescued at all, from the decrepitude into which it had fallen among debased dithyrambists and academic dramatists. Both of these forms of artificial poetry now quickly mouldered away. The dithyramb became a negligible form of poetry after Timotheus; of the tragic Pleiad of Alexandria the works were still-born and the very names are uncertain. By the middle of the third century B.C., or a little earlier, the new poetry, the elegy, had come into full possession, had set itself to rescue the salvage of poetry and, so far as might be possible, to refit and refloat the stranded vessel.

By his official position as well as by the volume and quality of his own writings, Callimachus was the recognised head among contemporary men of letters. Succeeding to the headship of the Alexandrian library after the brief occupancy of its first holder, Zenodotus, he held it for something like forty years. The position gave him the titular primacy of literature: it enabled him to organise and mould literary study, to gather round him associates and pupils, to found a school, and even, as happened with Apollonius, to proscribe and drive into a sort of literary exile any other poet who raised the standard of revolt against his authority. But he gained and held this sort of dictatorship not merely through his official position and the court favour gained him by his adroit flattery of the reigning house. His position rested also, as Dryden's did in England, on accomplished mastery of his art. *Elegiac princeps habetur Callimachus*, the terse phrase of Quintilian, expresses the fact that he was the head of the new poetry. Learning and high technical skill were united in him with real poetical genius. The author of the περὶ Ὕψους calls him ἄπτωτος, "the Faultless": he was the Andrea del Sarto of an age which had no Raffaele and no Michael Angelo. His poetry, like all the poetry of his period, was highly artificial; but then all poetry is highly artificial. The sneer of a Roman critic, "Read Callimachus if you wish not to know yourself," is levelled not at any particular artificiality, but against art: its point of view is that which looks on poetry not as an end but as a means, as a handbook to practice, not as a function of life.

The object of the new poetry, of the elegy, was to get poetry back into some kind of relation with what really, here and now, interested people—what people really cared for and thought and felt. In a world where all old boundaries had been broken up, where all old ideals had receded into the distance, which was floating in strange seas without chart or pilot, anything beyond a partial and fragmentary success in this task was impossible. The shipwreck of Hellenic life had left the miraculous and splendid achievement of Hellenic poetry more of an obsession than an inspiration. The price that has to be paid by the world for great art is that it overshadows and checks new growth.

Once the fullest expression of life, and still retaining indefinitely, even for distant ages and remote countries, its vitality and vivifying power, it lies on the generations which stand next to it with a weight heavy as frost. When we are disposed to think of the Callimachean elegy as something merely academic, we should not forget that among the most characteristic utterances of Callimachus are his attacks on academicism; on "those cyclic fellows"[1]—in the phrase used, much in his spirit, by a later poet of the school—who wrote lifeless poetry, imitative in substance and conventional in diction. He was the founder, or at least the establisher, of a new convention himself; but what is most important about it historically is not that it was academic, but that it was new.

This is so even with what is most academic in his extant work, the five hymns. These are an adaptation of an old form to new uses; they are really official odes, and, like all official odes—even those written by greater poets, by Horace or by Tennyson—have a heavy and formal quality, scarcely redeemed by their high finish or by their particular beauties of detail. At the end of the Hymn to Apollo is the celebrated passage in which Callimachus defends his own poetical method, one of fastidious selection and concentration. The draught that he offers, he says, is a quintessential distilment, *ἄκρον ἄωτον*: a small trickle of water, but from a sacred fountain, pure and unsullied.

[1] Pollianus in *Anth. Pal.*, xi. 130. The author of this epigram probably belongs to the neo-Alexandrian revival of the second century A.D.

The word, in this use, and the idea on which it is based, are taken by him from Pindar: *σοφίας ἄωτον ἄκρον κλυταῖς ἐπέων ῥοαῖσι ζυγέν*—"the essential distilment of wisdom linked with the lordly streams of poetry"—this is the quality of the work for which Pindar, in the seventh Isthmian, claims the sole right to immortality. Both poets held themselves haughtily aloof from the crowd; they set themselves to impose, not to follow, a fashion, to conquer rather than to woo fame. In the Hymns of Callimachus there are often phrases and passages which bear out the claim and substantiate the description.

> *πολλάκις ἐκ Τροιζῆνος ἀλιξάντοιο πολίχνης*
> *ἐρχόμενοι Ἐφύρηνδε Σαρωνικοῦ ἔνδοθι κόλπου*
> *ναῦται ἐπεσκέψαντο· καὶ ἐξ Ἐφύρης ἀνιόντες*
> *οἱ μὲν ἔτ' οὐκ ἴδον αὖθι.*

"Often from Troezen the sea-crumbled little town, going to Ephyre, within the Saronic Gulf, sailors sighted it: and returning from Ephyre, they no longer saw it there." Like that mysterious floating island, the vision of poetry comes to Callimachus in glimpses and then disappears. The quality for which the Hymns may still be prized lies in these glimpses, in the fine and sometimes even exquisite vignettes of incident or scenery. Like those of Horace, they have a curious effect of detachment; they stand out sharp in a glittering atmosphere, and the interstices between them, as with Horace, are carefully and painstakingly filled in with a deliberate workmanship that economises, refines, and arranges a material reduced to narrow limits by the author's fastidiousness, by an instinct for rejection which almost amounts to a passion.

In the epigram, this instinct can have full play; and the epigrams of Callimachus are not only his best work, but work which can be set beside the best of any period. Two hundred years earlier, when lyric poetry had already begun to harden, this form of poetry had been carried to its highest perfection in the hands of Simonides. In the long roll of the Greek epigrammatists, a succession which extends from first to last over no less than fifteen or sixteen hundred years, Callimachus is perhaps the second name. In both poets, it is the epitaph in which this form of poetry reaches its most complete perfection. The sepulcral epigrams of Callimachus have not only the fineness of the best Greek workmanship, but a depth of restrained feeling, a clear grave beauty, which makes them, in the full meaning of the words, both Hellenic and classic. In them at least his own claim for his poetry is justified; for in them the elegy, going back to its sources, has been able to fill these small cups with living water, distilled and translucent.

But it was the elegy in its larger scope which represented the main body of Callimachus' work, and by which he gave so marked a direction to the development of later poetry. In this sense the elegy means anything written in elegiac verse; and elegiac verse was the chosen medium for the new poetry. In the hands of the early Alexandrians it became a medium of quite extraordinary flexibility and scope. Even the English decasyllabic couplet hardly approaches it in plasticity

In Greek, when once its mechanism had been mastered, it almost writes itself. In Latin it had to be adapted, with immense labour and skill, to the refractory medium of a language whose native rhythms were alien from it; but even so, it became, and remained, the really dominant form for poetry. The heroic hexameter stood a little aloof and apart: poetry that dealt, or professed to deal, with life more directly was written in elegiacs. The profound effect of its predominance lasted right down to modern times. The chief intellectual occupation of the Middle Ages, it has been said with some truth, was writing enormous quantities of bad Latin verse; and the bulk of that verse was in elegiacs. The same is true of the Renaissance, except that the verse then ceased to be bad. In all the arts, substance and medium have an organic interconnection; and the forms of the Callimachean or Alexandrian elegy as transplanted into Latin have affected the whole development and progress of European poetry.

Callimachus, like his contemporaries, applied the new vehicle to a great variety of subject matter. His work extended over both of the two provinces specifically represented by the names of Euphorion and Aratus; that of amatory or sentimental poetry on the one hand, and that of scientific or quasi-scientific poetry on the other. It treated largely of history and archaeology, the romance of the Greek past as it was conceived by an age in which the romantic spirit was feeble and heavily overweighted by scholarship. It seems also to have taken a large range over the field of personal life. But except for the epigrams his elegiac verse is nearly all lost. The *Loutra Pallados,* a piece of less than 150 lines, is the only substantial fragment which survives. Beyond this his elegies are only known to us indirectly from Latin imitations. One of these, the *Coma Berenices* of Catullus, is not merely an imitation but a careful and close translation; and it enables us to some extent to see how in this kind of poetry Callimachus followed the middle path between sentimentally romantic and drily scientific treatment with adroit skill and with an accent of delicate irony. The *Loutra Pallados* shows poetical power of a remarkable kind. The workmanship of the trained artist is combined in it with a more intimate imaginative quality in lines and phrases, "jewels five words long," like the sudden and sonorous *συρίγγων ἀΐω φθόγγον ὑπαξόνιον;* or the beautiful picture flashed out in four words, like a phrase of Horace at his best, of the midday stillness on Helicon, "the sleep that is among the lonely hills" where Teiresias meets the goddess—*μεσαμερινὰ δ' εἶχ' ὄρος ἁσυχία*: or in whole passages like the wail of Chariclo—

> τί μοι τὸν κῶρον ἔρεξας
> πότνια; τοιαῦται δαίμονες ἐστὲ φίλαι;
> ὄμματά μοι τῶ παιδὸς ἀφείλεο· τέκνον ἄλαστε
> εἶδες Ἀθαναίας στάθεα καὶ λαγόνας,
> ἀλλ' οὐκ ἀέλιον πάλιν ὄψεαι· ὢ ἐμὲ δειλάν,
> ὢ ὄρος, ὢ Ἑλικών, οὐκ ἔτι μοι πάριτε·
> ἦ μεγάλ' ἀντ' ὀλίγων ἐπράξαο· δόρκας ὄλεσσας
> καὶ πρόκας οὐ πολλάς, φάεα παιδὸς ἔχεις.

Swinburne's rendering in his *Tiresias,* sympathetic and faithful as it is, comes short, as all translations must, of communicating the full poetical quality of the original—

> O holiest, what thing hast thou done,
> What, to my child? woe's me that see the thing!
> Is this thy love to me-ward, and hereof
> Must I take sample how the Gods can love?
>
> O child, thou hast seen indeed, poor child of mine,
> The breasts and flanks of Pallas bare in sight,
> But never more shalt see the dear sun's light.
> O Helicon, how great a pay is thine!
> For some poor antelopes and wild-deer dead,
> My child's eyes hast thou taken in their stead.

In this same poem, too, we can see, better perhaps than in any other surviving specimen, the delicate intonation, the long periodic movement, the sustained harmonies of which the Greek elegiac was capable in a master-hand. The creation of verse of such quality, such melody and cadence, was in itself a high poetic achievement. Among the Latins, Propertius alone mastered, or all but mastered, its secret. It died with him; but the conquest which the elegiac made of half the field of Latin poetry shows clearly how alluring and entrancing its effect was upon the Italian ear as well as on the Italian imagination.

II

THEOCRITUS AND THE IDYL

In speaking of the progress of Greek poetry after Athens, I have laid special stress on a fact which lies at the root of any real appreciation of what that poetry was, of what it meant to do, and what it did. The Alexandrian school of the third century B.C., using that term in its largest meaning, was occupied with a single task. Its object was to get poetry back into relation with life. The older Greek poets had become the classics. The life which they interpreted was now the life of a past world. That world disappeared in the fourth century B.C. The new and larger world which had absorbed and effaced it had to find its own poetry, had to express itself if it could in the forms of a new art. The task was one of infinite complexity and difficulty. For the centre of life had been lost. The Macedonian conquests threw it adrift. In the vast military monarchies which parcelled out among themselves a superficially Hellenised world, there was nowhere any real centre, nowhere any clear ideal. A new imaginative interpretation of life was sought with great assiduity in many directions. It was nowhere completely found; and even in the golden age of Alexandrianism, the age of Callimachus and Euphorion and Aratus, the Alexandrians are not classics in the full sense. They did what they could, and handed over the task for completion to another language, a separate race, a different genius. Rome conquered and annexed the Alexandrian kingdoms; and the Roman genius, building on the laborious Alexandrian foundations, produced the Latin classics.

But when we say that the Alexandrian age produced no classics, one exception is generally made, and not without reason. Theocritus, alike in histories of literature, in the general working estimate of scholars, and in the appreciation of lovers of poetry, is included in the roll of the classical Greek poets. He did once more for the last time what the artistry of the Greek genius had done so often in its great days; he created, and brought to perfection, a new kind of poetry, which alike in form and substance presented a new pattern of life. Before him, the pastoral, in the full sense of the term, hardly existed: after him and down to the present day, it has been a substantive form of poetry, co-ordinate with the epic and romance, with the lyric and the drama. And that form has been more than once of the utmost importance in the general evolution of poetry; in Virgil and the Virgilians; in the poetry of the romantic Middle Ages; in the later sixteenth century throughout Western Europe; and in the whole of that more modern poetry which derives from the sixteenth century by direct inheritance.

The name which represents most fully the central force and movement of Alexandrian poetry is not

Theocritus, but Callimachus. The two poets were contemporaries, and both were really working on kindred lines and with the same object. But Callimachus is not a living poet in the same sense as Theocritus is. Partly this is due to the mere fact —the accidental fact, as we say of things for which we cannot assign any definite reason—that so little of his work is extant, and so large a proportion of that little is not Callimachus at his best. But the main reason is one more vital; it is that the genius of Theocritus, in ranging over the field of life, as all the Alexandrians did, to rediscover and reincarnate poetry, struck on and seized the specific province of the pastoral. He saw the value of this new method; he developed it with immense skill and beauty. And so, while he is properly speaking an idylist, and while half of his extant poetry is not pastoral at all, it is as a pastoral poet, as the first and greatest of the pastoral poets, that he is universally and rightly known. In him the pastoral became classic: and that was the last transmutation which the spirit of poetry took fully and with complete success in Greek hands before she passed westward from the Greek world.

The Greek world and the Roman world are different worlds poetically just as they were different in history. But in both cases they overlap and intermingle; and in both cases the Greater Greece beyond the seas, as it was called with a sort of accidental prophecy, Sicily and Southern Italy, was where their boundaries first intersected. It has always been the fortune of Sicily, from its mere geographical position, like that of an eddy at the conflux of meeting tides, to occupy an ambiguous but cardinal place in the history of civilisation. It became a link, a stepping-stone, between Greece and Rome: and once more, in the strange revolutions of history, was a seed-ground many centuries later; for it was there that the complex hybridisation took place among Norman, Arab, and Italian elements which gave the decisive impulse towards the creation of Italian poetry in the hands of Dante and his successors. In the history of ancient poetry, the pastoral is its one specific and unique creation. But long before the time of Theocritus the Sicilian genius had been a factor in that history of no small importance. Just at the centre of the lyric age and before the vital energies of Greek poetry had concentrated on Athens, Stesichorus and the school of poets who bore his name appear, so far as can be judged from the few surviving fragments and the scanty notices of later writers, to have gone far, and in a very curious way, towards anticipating the work of the Alexandrians. Stesichorus himself was definitely a precursor of Theocritus. He remoulded the material of the epic under an idyllic or quasi-lyrical treatment. Among his poems are quoted instances of nearly all the kinds, other than the pastoral, which are extant in Theocritus' own works: encomia, epithalamia, epyllia, erotica; and even the pastoral itself seems to have taken its beginnings, in some sense, with him. His *Daphnis* is only a name, but there is evidence enough to assure us that it is the name of one who was the direct ancestor of the Theocritean figure—the patron saint, one might call him, of the Sicilian pastoral—which reappears in Theocritus himself, and in Virgil.

Even when the main impulse of poetry concentrated itself on Athens, the Sicilian school continued a separate existence and retained a native individuality. Aeschylus, Simonides, Pindar, all found their way to the court of Syracuse, not only because of the material rewards it offered, but because they found there a rich literary culture, a stimulating poetical atmosphere. Throughout the fifth century B.C. the Sicilian drama, in the comedies of Epicharmus and the mimes of Sophron and Xenarchus, was working on independent lines towards a popular realistic art which bore affinity to Italian no less than to Greek. Epicharmus, though he spent most of his life at the Sicilian Megara or at Syracuse, was born in Cos, the Dorian island which was the home, or one of the homes, possibly the birthplace and certainly the poetical school, of Theocritus himself; and which curiously enough became also, long afterwards, the home of one who has been called the last of the Greek poets, the Syrian Meleager.

Stesichorus was the first of the romantics, Sophron the first of the realists; or at least we may say so in order to emphasise their quality, if we take care to remember that such generalisations are always much too sweeping. This was the specific impress of Sicily upon Greek poetry; and in Theocritus it is the subtle intermixture of the two qualities which gives his poetry its peculiar charm and its vast historical importance. The return to nature took with him as with his contemporaries two forms. First, it was a sustained attempt to translate the old motives, the traditional subjects, of poetry into modern terms, to re-create or re-envisage them in the surroundings of modern art, modern surroundings, a modern attitude towards life. Secondly, it was an attempt which they all to some degree shared, but which Theocritus pursued with more skill and felicity than the rest, to bring the common things of life, its occupations, studies, amusements, the middle-class range of thought and sentiment and emotion, within the sphere of poetry. The note of the whole Alexandrian period is the emergence of the middle classes. Wealth and commerce were diffused; art was popularised; science, physical, historical, and mental, was widely cultivated. Government had passed into the hands of trained bureaucracies. Hellas had created the state and the individual, and had perished in the task. Life was thrown back upon itself to find fresh motives and outlets. The morning-glories, the ardours of midday were over. Poetry had to find new patterns, had to attach itself as it could to a life that lay, swarming and monotonous, flat amid immense horizons, in the endless aimless afternoon.

Poetry had to do this or die. The new world of the Hellenistic monarchies was a misfit; the times, in that metaphor of Hamlet's which is so perpetually quoted that it has almost lost all definite meaning, were out of joint, and the dislocation had to be reduced before the organism could reassume its functions. The sudden expansion of the Greek world had been effected through a process which left every joint racked.

Throughout Theocritus, explicitly in the more personal poems, here and there in vivid touches among them all, we feel the bewildering sense, the overwhelming pressure, of an over-expanded world. The wealth of the East was pouring into Europe through Egypt and Syria. The states of Greater Greece overseas were in fierce competition with Carthage for the control of the immense commerce of the West, in which the Roman Republic, now the mistress of Central Italy, was stretching downward and outward to claim its share. The world was externally governed by the rulers of vast states controlling huge trained armies; what ultimately governed these was the growing power of the plutocracy. Population was aggregated in swollen cities, and the *latifundia* were everywhere becoming the dominant feature of the world outside the cities. The scene painted by a dexterous hand, whether that of Theocritus or not, in the twenty-fifth Idyl, the *Heracles Leontophonos*, though laid in Elis, is not a picture of the Elis of small country squires like Xenophon; it is that of a *latifundium* in the full sense, an immense stretch of tillage and pasturage cultivated by slaves, who "live in long rows of huts, guarding the great and unspeakable wealth of their master." "All this plain," says the ploughman, "is held by Augeias, wheat-bearing tilth and orchards and uplands, over all which lands we go labouring the whole day long as thralls have to do." At evening "the cattle come in, ten thousand upon ten thousand, showing for multitude like the watery clouds that roll forward in heaven, and countless are they and ceaseless in their passage: the whole plain was filled and all the driftways. None would have deemed or believed that the substance of one man could be so vast."[1] Syracuse, the centre of Sicilian poetry, had grown to its utmost height of wealth, population, and splendour. Sixty thousand immigrants had poured into it after the downfall of the despotism of Dionysius II., and it grew more and more prosperous and wealthy through the long reign of Hiero, which was devoted throughout to the task of its material development, under a commercial and economic system unrivalled till then in the ancient world. Alexandria, the chief centre of the new poetry as it was of the whole intellectual life of the period, was, like ancient Babylon or Nineveh, or modern London, the metropolis of a vast empire. It had a population approaching a million. The dominions of Ptolemy Philadelphus stretched up into the Aegean, and southward "ten leagues beyond man's life," far into the mysterious Sudan, to lands "whence," in Theocritus' own vivid phrase, "the Nile is no longer visible."[2] "Countless are the lands, and tribes of men innumerable win increase of the soil, waxing under the rain of God. All the sea and land and sounding rivers are under the sway of Ptolemy; many are his horsemen, many his footmen that march gleaming in bronze under shield; and in wealth he outweighs all kings."[3] Ptolemy, according to the prose records of historians, maintained an army as large as that of the whole Roman empire; two hundred thousand

[1] Theocr. xxv. 23–25, 29–33, 88–97, 115–117.

[2] Theocr. vii. 114, *πέτρᾳ ὕπο Βλεμύων, ὅθεν οὐκέτι* Νεῖλος *ὁρατός*.

[3] Theocr. xvii. 77 foll.

infantry, forty thousand cavalry, war-chariots and war-elephants, fifteen hundred sail of the line. He left £200,000,000 in the treasury at his death; and this was after a reign of lavish and continuous expenditure. The description of the splendours of the yearly Adonis-festival of Alexandria, provided at the royal expense, in the *Adoniazusae* idyl, falls far short of the historical record given by Callixenus[1] of a coronation feast. It fatigues the imagination by its picture of overwhelming wealth and magnificence.

Commerce and peace—the peace that commerce secures for itself when politics are the business of court chancelleries and war has become a paid profession—had made intercommunication easy throughout the Mediterranean world and far beyond it. Nationality almost ceased to exist. We cannot tell with most of the poems of Theocritus whether they were written in Sicily, or in Cos, or at Alexandria. A voyage from Syracuse to Miletus is spoken of in the twenty-eighth Idyl as quite an ordinary thing. In the fourth, mention is casually made of a herdsman going off from his pasture in Southern Italy to visit the Olympic games. In the fourteenth—the scene here is probably also in Southern Italy, but unidentifiable—the company of four who meet for a merry-making include an Argive, a Thessalian from Larissa, and a mercenary who has no country at all and is merely called "the soldier." One of the interlocutors, who is in despair because his young woman has, for quite sufficient reason, run away from him, is recommended to

[1] Quoted by Athenaeus, v. 25–35.

the Latin *species* has come down to us in the word *spice*. A book of idyls was simply a collection of poems on a small scale, finely wrought and precious. The idea is the same as was in the minds of our Elizabethans, only expressed by them with their usual exorbitance of language, when they gave collections such titles as a *Gorgeous Gallery of Gallant Inventions*, or a *Paradise of Dainty Devices*, or a *Banquet of Dainty Conceits;* or it is a variant of the common metaphor by which (as in the *Emaux et Camées* of Théophile Gautier) poetry of this sort is described in the terms of jewellery. A nearer analogy still may perhaps be found in the art of painting. Idyllia are cabinet-pictures; small in size, highly finished, detachable, not imagined and executed as elements in any large constructive scheme of imaginative decoration, yet each holding its tiny convex mirror up to nature, each bringing art for a moment into relation with one facet or mood of life.

Greek criticism had, with that just instinct which makes so many of its judgments permanently valid, distinguished three main kinds of poetry: lyric, epic, and dramatic. The idyllic method, in the hands of Theocritus, was applied to the material of all three, following to a considerable extent at least the specific bent which had been given to each by his Sicilian predecessors. His epic idyls derive in spirit from Stesichorus, both being based on the romantic and modern treatment of scenes from the traditional body of epic story. His dramatic idyls derive similarly from the native Sicilian drama, the comedies and the mimes. There are also idyls in the collection which are lyrical or quasi-lyrical. But between these and the dramatic idyls there is no certain line of demarcation. All poetry which deals with emotion tends to become lyrical; and all poetry which deals with action tends to become dramatic. We speak habitually and quite rationally of the lyrical quality of scenes in a drama or even passages in a narrative poem; and no less so of the dramatic quality of both lyrics and epics.

Upon this groundwork then, already so complex, Theocritus superinduced two more factors: first the elegiac, the poetry of reflection and sentiment, which was common to him with his whole age—the elegy, as I have already said, being the specific central form in which the main current of Alexandrian poetry ran—and secondly his own creation, the pastoral. All these are intertwined, shot through, fused into a poetical product of singularly varied, elusive, and iridescent beauty, χαριέστερον τῇ ποικιλίᾳ, in the apt words of an ancient commentator. But also throughout his work—and this is what makes him the last of the Greek classics—there is the fineness of edge, the purity of line, the delicate precision of modelling, which are the qualities of authentic Greek art.

When Tennyson, in issuing his collected poems, gave the general title of English Idyls to the pieces which he added to the second volume of the Poems of 1842 and to some others in the same manner written or published later, he used the name (as he used language always) with precise accuracy and with a

It pleased me well enough. 'Nay, nay,' said Hall,
'Why take the style of those heroic times?
For nature brings not back the Mastodon,
Nor we those times; and why should any man
Remodel models? these twelve books of mine
Were faint Homeric echoes, nothing-worth.'

How far this passage represents actual fact, how far merely the thoughts that passed through Tennyson's mind, is irrelevant. The fact remains that the scene or episode, treated in the idyllic manner, and thus brought into a fresh relation alike to the older poetry and to the life of the modern world, is what the early Alexandrian and the early Victorian poet alike instinctively sought after as the substance of a new poetry.

When Tennyson resumed or continued the subject, it was still in the idyllic mode of treatment. *The Idyls of the King* is a title carefully chosen and significant. He finally wrought them into a more or less complete cycle, not a single poem even then, but a single body of poetry—or so he wished them to be—*The Idyls of the King, in Twelve Books,* according to the title which he finally gave them himself. But an idyllic cycle is not an epic. The idyl and the epic are at the two opposite ends of the world of poetry; it is a sort of symbol of this that Greek classical poetry begins with the one and ends with the other.

The lines of prologue and epilogue between which the *Morte d'Arthur* is framed are also just such as Theocritus might have written; not least the curious line in the epilogue about "King Arthur like a modern gentleman." The attempt in both cases is to give new life to poetry by bringing the subjects of poetry into a fresh touch with the actual modern world. In both cases it was an attempt made rather wearily, and after all with imperfect success so far as its main object was concerned.

Even the words in which the two poets express themselves with regard to the function of their own poetry, its possibilities, its limitations, its discouragements, are often remarkably alike, sometimes all but identical. In the sixteenth idyl, the *Hiero*, Theocritus, speaking in his own person, expresses himself with regard to modern poetry exactly, down to very turns of phrase, as Tennyson does over and over again. For both the Muses speak "with darkened brow"—σκυζόμεναι—or sit silent with heads bowed over chill knees and unshod feet. "I was born too late," cries the poet in the *Golden Year*—

> A tongue-tied poet in the feverous days
> That, setting the how much before the how,
> Cry, like the daughters of the horse-leech, "Give":

echoing the words of his Greek predecessor, οὐ γὰρ ἔτ' ἄνδρες ὡς πάρος ἐσθλοῖς αἰνεῖσθαι σπεύδοντι, νενίκηνται δ' ὑπὸ κερδέων. To both it seemed in their moods of discouragement, "far better to be born to labour and the mattock-hardened hand," ὡσεί τις μακέλᾳ τετυλωμένος ἔνδοθι χεῖρας. "The love of letters, overdone, had swamped the sacred poets with themselves": there was no welcome for them left: τίς δέ κεν ἄλλου ἀκούσαι; ἅλις πάντεσσιν Ὅμηρος. Yet that discouragement was only a mood, and they felt the joy of their art. "But we," Tennyson says in the epilogue to the *Morte d'Arthur*,

> Sat rapt: it was the tone with which he read—
> Perhaps some modern touches here and there
> Redeem'd it from his charge of nothingness—
> Or else we loved the man and prized his work.

So too Theocritus strikes the same note: *ἐς δὲ καλεύντων θαρσήσας Μοίσαισι σὺν ἁμετέραισιν ἰοίμαν*—"To those who welcome me will I come in courage, with the poetry that is mine."[1]

This is already a digression, or would be so were it not that all poetry is one thing, being the interpretation and pattern of one thing, life. But it would be delightful to carry the digression on, and point out the analogies, subtle or patent, between the Theocritean and the Tennysonian manner and treatment. Both poets have the same kind of sense of language; the same enriched and loaded sweetness of phrasing; the same sensitiveness to sights and sounds. The work of both is occasionally irradiated by the same romantic, almost mystical, passion for beauty. It is in the epic idyls, and the genre-pieces, if I may use with an apology a term for which there is scarcely an exact English equivalent, that these analogies are most striking; for the pastorals proper are a kind of poetry in which Theocritus, though he has had many followers, has never had a quite authentic colleague. The thirteenth idyl, the *Hylas*, is full of examples: we may notice especially the enriched detail in purely subsidiary description: "Neither at midday nor at dawn, nor

[1] Idyl xvi. 8, 11, 15, 20, 32, 106–7.

when twittering chickens look for bed-time, and their mother has ruffled out her wings on the dusty perch"—

οὐδ' ὁπόκ' ὀρτάλιχοι μινυροὶ ποτὶ κοῖτον ὁρῷεν
σεισαμένας πτερὰ ματρὸς ἐπ' αἰθαλόεντι πετεύρῳ—

the minute particularity in the list of flowers that grow about the pool—

περὶ δὲ θρύα πολλὰ πεφύκει
κυάνεόν τε χελιδόνιον χλωρόν τ' ἀδίαντον
καὶ θάλλοντα σέλινα καὶ εἰλιτενὴς ἄγρωστις—

"About it grew rushes many and glossy celandine and green maidenhair and lush cow-parsley and marsh couch-grass": and the swift-flashing phrase of the girl "with Spring in her eyes"—ἔαρ ὁρόωσα—followed immediately by the elaborately expanded simile of the falling star: "As when a star shoots flaming out of heaven and flashes down into the sea, and one cries to his fellow-sailors, Up with the tackling, lads, lightly: the wind is fair for sailing":

ἀθρόος ὡς ὅτε πυρσὸς ἀπ' οὐρανοῦ ἤριπεν ἀστὴρ
ἀθρόος ἐν πόντῳ, ναύταις δέ τις εἶπεν ἑταίροις·
κουφότερ' ὦ παῖδες ποιεῖσθ' ὅπλα· πλευστικὸς οὖρος.[1]

All these are in the specifically idyllic manner which we may call indifferently Theocritean or Tennysonian.

What I have called the realism or modernism of Theocritus runs through the whole of his work. It is sometimes most striking in poems where the poetic

[1] Idyl xiii. 11–12, 40–2, 50–2.

artifice, the idyllic convention, is most strongly marked. His effort after realism issued in a form of poetry which has become the very type of unreality. But the truth is that what is called realism in art is after all only a new convention; it is of the essence of art that it is not nature, but an interpretation, a reconstitution of nature. The felicity of his genius is most apparent in the skill and dexterity of touch by which he gets his poetic convention into tone with the naturalistic modern touches that he incorporates with it. He even uses these so as to convey into his poetry a fresh accent of strangeness and romance. Current phrases of the populace, whether town or country folk, even now and then pieces of popular slang, are so used and so reset by him as to bring out some vivid latent colour which in ordinary usage had long become dull and blurred. He had something of the genius of Burns in rehandling, and by slight touches transfiguring, what, before he took it in hand, had been commonplace, vulgar, empty of beauty. What he touched he rekindled. An instance is a phrase in the song of Battus in the tenth idyl, over which translators have stumbled badly: *πόδες ἀστράγαλοί τευς*, says the reaper to the flute-girl who has stolen his heart away. Somehow or other the words are filled with an indefinable elusive beauty. Mr. Lang in translating the idyl felt the beauty—he could not otherwise—but could only reproduce it by transposing it into the key of courtly romance: "Thy feet are fashioned like carven ivory," he renders it. They that have feet like carven ivory wear soft raiment and are in kings' houses; there is not a word of carven ivory in the Greek. The language of Battus, here and throughout his song, is that of a common rustic, with little gift of expression, whose rudimentary imagination half expresses itself in clumsy metaphors. "I'm sure," says Tony Lumpkin while he is pretending to make love to Miss Neville in Goldsmith's play, "I always loved cousin Con's pretty, long fingers, that she twists this way and that, over the haspicolls, like a parcel of bobbins." That is the tone of the Theocritean phrase. "Your feet are knucklebones," says Battus; and Theocritus takes the crude phrase as it stands, makes it vivid, makes it poetry. He conveys into it not merely the whole picture of the thin brown feet leaping and falling to the rattle of anklet-rings as the body sways and the voice drones above them, but a sense of some inner beauty, some touch of romance and almost of magic.

Once at least, it is curious to note, Theocritus falls into the same sort of mistake himself. In the long description of the carving on the cup in the first idyl—thirty lines of elaborate pictorial treatment—he forgets the quality of pastoral, and of his own genius. *Théocrite décrit rarement pour décrire,* says a French critic very justly; and this passage is one of three or four only of this kind in his whole volume. In that first idyl he is feeling his way towards his perfect manner; he has not yet fully learned how much to reject. The picture within the picture breaks the illusion; and incidentally he represents the shepherd's ivy-wood cup, bought by him for a goat and cheese, as decorated in a way that would only be possible, if at all, to carry out in laborious orient ivory with fabulous expense. Realism which has lost touch with reality is merely futile.

Or take another instance of the way in which Theocritus catches little ordinary phrases, words of common talk, and makes poetry of them. In the wonderful monologue of Simaetha in the second idyl there is a phrase that has something of the same wild magic beauty as there is in the song of Battus. "Now that I am alone," says the girl, "I will begin to go over it all. First it was the fair of St. Artemis; I borrowed a neighbour's gown and went out to see the shows, and a string of wild beasts were paraded, and there was a lioness"—ἐν δὲ λέαινα. Just what any common girl might say, as her shallow mobile brain flitted over little pointless incidents that came into her memory; but the three words—I almost despair of conveying the impression they make; one either feels it or does not—take under the poet's touch a strangeness and suggestiveness that make their cadence ring long in the mind, a gleam that will not leave them.

The sense of romance, inwoven through all or nearly all the idyls through slight, almost imperceptible touches, seldom gathers to any volume or high pressure. It does so, however, in one poem, the twelfth idyl, the *Aïtes*, or, as one might translate it into Elizabethan English, the Passionate Pilgrim. Here the romance, as in Shakespeare's Sonnets, is interfused with a strange half-mystical passion. It is full of phrases which are startlingly like those of the Sonnets: "The world-without-end hour whilst I, my sovereign, watch the clock for you"; "So are you to my thoughts as food to life or as sweet-seasoned showers are to the ground"; "In him those holy antique hours are seen"; "A backward look even of five hundred courses of the sun"; "Nor shall Death brag thou wanderest in his shade when in eternal lines to time thou growest"; "You still shall live, such virtue hath my pen, where breath most breathes, even in the mouths of men"; "So I return rebuked to my content, and gain by ills thrice more than I have spent."

That charged, enriched, self-conscious passion is at one extreme of Theocritus' genius; at the other extreme are his scenes of realistic comedy, with their extraordinary fidelity to life, yet with a thread of music in them that just makes them poetry. The fifteenth idyl, the *Adoniazusae,* is too well known to need being dwelt on; but it is worth noting, as an instance of its immense skill, how Praxinoa's most gorgeous outburst of vulgarity comes immediately before the Adonis-song with its wonderful opening imagery of the soft-footed Hours, the Hours that are so slow and so dear, that always come bringing gifts: yet the genius of the artist is such that he manages to keep the two passages in tone. To this side of his work too belongs that fourteenth idyl which I have already cited, with its literal transcript of the dull featureless provincial life—like the life in which Burns grew up, we might say again—which drove its young men, from sheer ennui, either to drink or to the recruiting sergeant.

I have dwelt somewhat at length on the great range of Theocritus' poetical method and invention, because it was largely in virtue of this that he became a force in poetry. But it is in his own central field, in the pastoral, that his unique poetical achievement lies. It is here that he brought to the life of a rather weary and dispirited age a draught of translucent freshness: in his own lovely phrase, "a cup washed in the wells of the Hours." Ἁδύ τι, "sweetness," is the key-word of the pastorals; the delicate sweetness of nature as it appealed to senses still unclouded but now transmitting their impressions to a new and exquisite sensibility. Ἁδύ τι τὸ ψιθύρισμα—"sweet and low"—the note is struck with a sort of soft certainty in the very first words of the first idyl. Κοῦφον δέ τι τοῦτο καὶ ἀδὺ γίνετ' ἐπ' ἀνθρώπως, εὑρεῖν δ' οὐ ῥᾴδιόν ἐστιν, he says again of his own poetry in the eleventh idyl, "delicate and sweet, and not easy to find." It was not easy; for no one else has ever quite found it again. Καὶ ἐς ὕστερον ἅδιον ᾀσω—"I will sing even sweeter yet"—are the last words of Thyrsis; and indeed Theocritus never exhausts his sweetness. The word runs like a thread of gold through the pastorals.

> Sweet is the whispering of the pine, and sweet
> The tinkle of the water at our feet,
> And sweet your piping, herder of the goats.

"Sweeter, O shepherd, is your song," replies the goatherd. "The sweet Cyprian" comes laughing; "sweet we murmured to one another," says the girl under the flooding moonlight; "sweet delight in kisses" is the longing of Amaryllis's lover; "sweet the piping" of "him who sat upon the rocks and fluted to the morning sea"; "sweet" the song of Comatas lying on the hill under the oaks and pines. "Sweet is the voice of the heifer, sweet her breath, and sweet to lie all night by running water in summer under the bare sky," Daphnis sings; and "sweet is your mouth, Daphnis," cries the admiring listener.

The discovery of this hitherto untouched sweetness in life was the triumph and glory of the pastoral. It made Sicily into a golden world; and it made all the world into Sicily. There is really very little direct evidence that Theocritus was a Sicilian poet by birth. "He was a Syracusan," says the entry under his name in the lexicon of Suidas, "or, as others say, a Coan settled in Syracuse." The epigram which makes him speak of himself as a Syracusan was written long after his time, and is of no authority. He identifies himself, more or less consciously, with his own singing shepherd, Thyrsis of Aetna, but that proves nothing. No doubt the scenery in several of the idyls—not really in many—is expressly Sicilian, and where it is so, it is spoken of with a sort of personal passion; the lyrical cry in the Αἴτνα μᾶτερ ἐμά of Menalcas' song in the ninth idyl sounds as if it came straight from the poet himself; in the song of Thyrsis in the first idyl he calls Pan as if in his own voice to leave Arcadia and its legendary hills, and "come hither to the Sicilian isle." But all we can say for certain is that both Sicily and Southern Italy were familiar to him, and that he certainly spent part of his life in both, in youth probably, in maturer years certainly. The scenery of the Italo-Sicilian idyls is sometimes that of Calabria rather than of Sicily: two or three are definitely placed in Italy; in the eighth, the shepherd looks down on the Sicilian sea from the "myriad depth" of what seems to be a Calabrian forest. But the scene of the *Thalysia* certainly, the loveliest of all the idyls, and I think also that of the *Pharmaceutriae,* the most passionate and splendid, is laid in Cos, which was not only an island of extreme beauty, but a school of poets: Philetas, his own immediate master, was a Coan. In Alexandria itself he must have lived long enough not only to be perfectly familiar with it—the *Adoniazusae* is sufficient proof of this, and nearly all men of letters in that golden age of Alexandrianism drifted to Alexandria—but to feel keenly, in its shadeless atmosphere and swarming life, home-sickness for the woods and streams and meadows of a more northern mountain land.

That home-sickness is the note of pastoral. Its return to nature is the return of tired men to their childhood; young themselves in mind no longer, they find in natural beauty and in the simpler life of the open air the illusion, and something more than an illusion, of the fountain of youth. To see the fresh beauty of the natural world freshly, to feel it not merely through their bodily senses but through a medium of enriched art and long poetic tradition, to re-create it imaginatively, was the achievement of the pastoral poets.

Yon cloud with that long purple cleft
Brings fresh into my mind
A day like this which I have left
Full thirty years behind.

My eyes are dim with childish tears,
My heart is idly stirred,
For the same sound is in my ears
Which in those days I heard.

In all the Theocritean pastorals there is, expressed or implicit, this accent of yearning. Sometimes, as in the first or third idyls, it is explicit; sometimes it is hardly to be found in the words, only in the atmosphere. It is always felt in the verse, the lingering, soft-cadenced, frail bucolic hexameter. The "pathetic insincerity" which has been spoken of as characteristic of the pastoral is not really insincere. If it were, it would certainly not have the power, as it has, of moving, for generation after generation—*γενεῇς δὲ διηκοσίῃσιν ἔπειτα*—the heart of the world.

The emplacement and scope of pastoral are given, completely and once for all, in the *Thalysia.* Romance and realism are there fused into something different from either: as in the Venetian Pastoral of Giorgione, they merge in a tone and colour which are and are not those of life, and in which the distinctions of the older kinds of art are disappearing.

Let be:
Say nothing now unto her lest she weep,
Nor name this ever. Be it as it was:
Life touching lips with Immortality.

Like Giorgione, Theocritus had artistic predecessors, but no artistic parent. The "bucolic Muse" appears indeed, at the beginning of the first idyl, as a name already familiar; the name is old Sicilian, we are told, and goes back to Stesichorus. But in the sense in which it is an actual and accomplished art it is the creation of Theocritus. Before him, it has origins, but no history. After him it has history enough, but hardly any further development.

Theocritus has been called the most and least natural of the Greek poets: it is just because he was both that he was able to effect his wonderful creation, to fuse elements which in their very nature are anxious to leap asunder. The weakness of sentimental and romantic poetry is that sentiment blurs the impressions of the senses, and romance plays havoc with the intelligence. The sensitiveness to nature in Theocritus is like that of Shelley or Coleridge: only they or poets of a gift akin to theirs could have given us the "sea-green dawn"—γλαυκὰν ἠῶ—of the sixteenth idyl, or the south-easter (not, as on the Neapolitan or Tuscan coast, the west wind) that stirs the seaweed far below—ὃς ἔσχατα φυκία κινεῖ—in the seventh; and the dramatic idyls show an observation of life that is no less radiantly clear.

These gifts he did not transmit to his pupils; and immediately after him (so quick bright things come to confusion) the pastoral fell to pieces. Theocritus is original and Greek. Bion of Smyrna is imitative and Asiatic: as workmanship, adroit; as poetry, valueless. The "Sicilian song" which he professes to sing in the fragment of *Achilles and Deidameia*—if that piece be his, which is doubted—is neither a song nor Sicilian; the

Adonis-dirge is so uninspired that it suggests something produced by machinery. In Moschus, the third of the three bucolic poets who were admitted into the canon, the Theocritean tradition is alive, but on the point of dissolving. It makes a swan-like end, fading in music of extraordinary sweetness; only the sweetness is becoming deliquescent; the clear touch, the pure line, of classical art begin to disappear. His Muse moves among dreams before dawn such as that beautifully described in the opening lines of his *Europa:* "When the third watch of the night sets in and the dawn is near, when sleep sweeter than honey rests on the eyelids and relaxes the limbs, enchaining the eyes in soft fetters, when the nation of dreams that come true goes shepherded." [1]

Moschus is immortal as the author of one poem, the elegy on Bion. That lovely wail by the Sicilian waters, so unapproachable in its languorous but piercing beauty, so precious to us not only for its own sake but because it is the precursor and model of the *Lycidas* and the *Adonais* and the *Thyrsis*, is not only a lament for Bion; it is a lament for Greek poetry. "Tell the Sicilian waters that song has died, and the Dorian minstrelsy perished": *σὺν αὐτῷ καὶ τὸ μέλος τέθνακε καὶ ὤλετο Δωρὶς ἀοιδά.* "All the gifts of the Muses have died with thee": *πάντα τοι ὦ βούτα συγκάτθανε δῶρα τὰ Μοισᾶν.* The whole roll of the Greek poets is summoned to join in the lamentation, from Homer and Hesiod and Orpheus down through the line of the lyrists and elegists, Sappho and Pindar, Alcaeus and

[1] Mosch. ii. 2–5.

Anacreon and Archilochus, Asclepiades and Philetas; "and among the Syracusans Theocritus; but I sing thee the dirge of an Ausonian sorrow." It is this last line upon which the most stress is to be laid. For the light of poetry was passing from Hellas to Ausonia, and for Hellas there was to be no second spring. "Ah me, when the mallows wither in the garden, and the green parsley and the curled shoots of the anise, once more they spring again later and blow for another year; but we men the great and mighty, we the wise, when we have died the first time, go down into silence, and in the hollow land sleep well the very long termless unawakening sleep." The circle of the Greek poets was rounded off and returned into itself: the "Dorian Orpheus was perished." When this most musical of mourners wrote its epitaph in those lovely lines, the axis of the world had shifted. Sicily had become a Roman province. The streets of the white towns rang under the tramp of the terrible Latin infantry, and the Sicilian waters were swept by Latin fleets. Ennius and Plautus were creating a new poetry, full of the pride of a new life, at Rome; and the shepherds and ploughmen and fisher-folk of Theocritus were sinking into a wretched provincial proletariat, *minutus populus*, a people meted out and trodden down, the serf-population of the sovereign Republic.

Not indeed that the Theocritean pastoral was the last word in Greek poetry, or that in him Greek poetry wholly ended its creative energy. New methods were still being essayed; the impulse to get poetry into relation with life was not wholly exhausted. The romantic epic as it took shape, timidly and imperfectly, in the hands of Apollonius the Rhodian, was a germ destined to develop great things; of the two poets it is Apollonius and not Theocritus who had the larger and more decisive influence in suggesting and awakening the consummate art of Virgil. But Theocritus not only suggested a new art in poetry; he effectively created it, and left it complete. Not quite the last of the Greek poets, he is the last poet among the Greek classics. Apollonius and the rest are half-forgotten; Theocritus is alive. And this creation of his was his own, the product of his unique genius. He remains, even now, the supreme master of the pastoral; but even were it otherwise, we still might say, in the words placed in the mouth of the inventor of the tragic drama three hundred years earlier: "Younger generations refashion this, and infinite time will make many more discoveries yet; but mine are mine."[1] The opening phrase of the lines written in Theocritus' person and prefixed to the volume of his poems may be taken in a sense in which it was not meant, and so read as to be both a claim to and a judgment on his place among the poets: ἄλλος ὁ Χῖος· ἐγὼ δε Θεόκριτος —"Homer is different: I am Theocritus." With a backward look even of five hundred courses of the sun, the Idyls close the golden pomp which opened with the Iliad.

[1] Dioscorides on Thespis in *Anth. Pal.*, vii. 410.

III

APOLLONIUS OF RHODES AND THE ROMANTIC EPIC

ALEXANDRIANISM, as it worked itself out in the group of poets belonging to the former half of the third century before Christ, meant among other things the decisive predominance of the short poem. This is a common feature of the new art in its many essays along various lines of development; alike in the hymns and elegies of Callimachus, in the poetry of sentiment as represented by Philetas and Euphorion, in the poetry of science as represented by Aratus, and in the idyls and pastorals of Theocritus and his school. Their method, to whatever subject it might be applied, got its effects within short compass; more than that, it lost them, or tended to lose them, if that compass were much extended. The *Loutra Pallados* of Callimachus, a piece of less than one hundred and fifty lines, or the *Thalysia* of Theocritus, a piece of a little over one hundred and fifty, are about the normal maximum at which this kind of poetry completes its orbit. Where that limit is largely exceeded, the weaknesses of the method—or rather, perhaps, the weaknesses of the poets who used it—begin to show themselves. Their swallow-flights of song dip and skim; they have not power of wing for prolonged and continuous imaginative composition. Of the *Hecale* of Callimachus, a long poem as length was then counted, we have only a few fragments; but there is some reason to believe that it was a deliberate attempt to work on a scale which was beyond that which commended itself to his own judgment. The fragmentary *Heracles Leontophonos* of Theocritus produces, in something under three hundred lines, an effect approaching tediousness. Even in the necessarily larger scope of the scientific poem, the *Phaenomena* and *Diosemeia* of Aratus do not exceed the length of a normal single book of the Iliad and the Odyssey respectively. Lycophron's *Cassandra* would be tedious however short it were, but its tediousness is greatly exaggerated by its running to the length of about fifteen hundred lines. Much of the finest work of the period is to be found within the narrow limit of the epigram, and it was towards the epigram or something approximating to the epigram that the art of poetry seemed to be moving, at all events on the side on which it had the most certain vitality. That slight but real form of poetry remained alive when the other forms invented and practised by the Alexandrians dwindled away. The successors of Callimachus in elegy seem to have been for the most part feeble copyists: Nicander and the other didactic poets show a similar falling-off from Aratus; and we have seen how rapidly the pastoral idyl sank into silence or into futility after Theocritus.

The cult of the short poem became elevated into a dogma. It is crystallised in the saying attributed to

Callimachus, *μέγα βίβλιον μέγα κακόν*, "a big book is a great nuisance." Like most dogmas, it was the emphasised assertion of what could not be rationally proved; and it was not only emphasised, but polemical; it was directed against a school which asserted the contrary, and tried to justify their opinion not merely by criticism but by practice. What is true of the arts generally is true of poetry likewise, that the predominance of any one school or manner creates a reaction, which in the hands of able or ambitious artists becomes a revolt. Sometimes the revolt succeeds, and then it becomes a revolution.

The revolt against Alexandrianism was headed by Apollonius, called the Rhodian. It was sustained by him almost single-handed, and he had not the genius or the luck to make it succeed. I use the words genius and luck as though they were alternative causes of success, but this is hardly the case. *Τυχὴ τέχνην ἔστερξε καὶ τέχνη τυχήν*, as Agathon said in the line that Aristotle is so fond of quoting; and the Latin *felicitas* includes both. The failure of Apollonius in his revolt against the Alexandrian practice and the Callimachean dogma, so far as it failed—and for the time it did fail—was due to his infelicity. But felicity, according to the doctrine of the practical Roman mind, was not a mere chance product of external causes; it was also a virtue in its possessor. The virtue that was in the young rebel who at the age of less than twenty ran up his red flag in Alexandria itself and before the nose of the dictator of poetry was not powerful enough to dethrone the occupying dynasty. It was not even powerful enough to make him produce a great poem. But it was powerful enough to survive temporary defeat and to give a new direction afterwards to the main course of poetry. The effective result of Apollonius in the progress of poetry is to be found not in the *Argonautica* itself, and still less in any new development which Greek poetry took after him. He did not succeed in giving that poetry any new vitalising impulse; he did not even arrest its decline and decay. His effective result is to be found two hundred years afterwards in Virgil. He scarcely founded a school, but he had one transcendent scholar. Virgil studied all the Alexandrians deeply and plundered from them freely; but Apollonius he absorbed and transfigured by his own genius; it is not too much to say that but for the *Argonautica* we should not have had the Aeneid. He used Theocritus in some such way in the Eclogues; but in the Eclogues he had not mastered his own art, and the specific Virgilianism which gives them their charm and beauty is as yet intermittent and not under full control. He used Aratus in some such way in the Georgics, but Aratus is only a secondary influence in that wonderful texture. Theocritus and Aratus still stand by themselves—on very different poetical levels, it is true. But in the Aeneid Virgil not only absorbed Apollonius; he effaced him.

Still, the poem which had a germinal effect of so immense a significance clearly must require and repay study, even it were not the case, as it is the case, that it has a substantive beauty and value of its own. In poetry we must not look for what is not there; and in the *Argonautica* we need not look for either the classical or the romantic quality in anything approaching perfection. He is at once a classicist and a romanticist; he wavers between the two methods, unable and unwilling to rid himself fully of his classicism, unable and probably undesirous to launch out fully into his romanticism. He never merges or fuses the two into that supreme product which, to use once more a phrase which bears repetition, is neither classical nor romantic, but is simply right. "The imagination of a boy is healthy," Keats writes in the preface to *Endymion*, "and the mature imagination of a man is healthy; but there is a space of life between, in which the soul is in a ferment, the character undecided, the way of life uncertain, the ambition thick-sighted: thence proceeds mawkishness." When Apollonius conceived and executed the first draft of his *Argonautica*, he was in this state of ferment, between boy and man; his ambitions were thick-sighted, his way uncertain, the character he meant to give to poetry undecided. Only, he was not a Keats. Keats knew better than to spend the rest of his life in revising and rewriting *Endymion*. One cannot imagine Apollonius saying or thinking what Keats says in the same preface: "In this poem the reader must soon perceive great inexperience, immaturity, and every error denoting a feverish attempt rather than a deed accomplished. The two first books, and indeed the two last, I feel sensible are not of such completion as to warrant their passing the press; nor should they if

I thought a year's castigation would do them any good; it will not—the foundations are too sandy. It is just that this youngster should die away." What he did do was precisely the contrary. His poem had been received by the Quarterly Reviewers of the day with a storm of obloquy. He went away with his poem to Rhodes—somewhat as a modern French poet might remove from Paris to Brussels—and there devoted not one year but many, "the rest of his life" according to the vague generalities of scholiasts, to its castigation. How far this labour went in materially changing either the substance or the tone and handling of the poem is unfortunately quite unknown. But as it was devoted largely at least towards meeting the objections raised by his critics, it may be safely assumed that the result was something of a compromise between the legitimist and revolutionary principles. The remodelling of a poem by its author is rarely a success; life is apt to evaporate in the process. If we possessed the original *Argonautica*, we might very likely find it full of the faults of youth—crude, uneven, indecorous, sometimes setting our teeth on edge—but we should know better what Apollonius and his revolt meant, what they tried to do; and we probably might not find in it that fatal flatness, that mechanical polish, which is the condemnation of the existing poem. "I hope," Keats continues in that splendid preface, "I hope I have not in too late a day touched the beautiful mythology of Greece, and dulled its brightness." This is just what Apollonius, with all his merits, did; and this is what sets him, as regards substantive value though not as regards effect on poetry, below the Alexandrian poets of the earlier school.

A furious controversy raged for years between the two schools. Apollonius had the great advantage of being a generation younger; time was on his side; nor had he to fight single-handed. At the death of Callimachus, the chief librarianship of Alexandria was conferred on a man of science, a physicist and mathematician. This may perhaps, apart from the eminence of Eratosthenes, the greatest name in science of the whole Ptolemaic age, be taken as indicating that the supremacy of the Callimachean doctrine and practice was so much shaken that it did not survive Callimachus. An armed truce was imposed on the literary conflict. When Eratosthenes died a few years later, it was Apollonius himself who was called to fill his place. But he was not received into the Canon of Greek classics drawn up by Aristarchus. The truce issued in a compromise, where neither party could claim a decided victory.

The epic—if we use the word in its laxer and wider sense as meaning the long narrative poem—had dwindled away gradually in the earlier age of Hellenic literature. The bulk of the cyclic poets are dated in the eighth century B.C., but their successors continue in the seventh and even into the sixth. The rediscovery, the effective re-emergence of Homer in the sixth century was almost coincident with their disappearance. But between them and the new movement of the third century there is not a complete gap. Narrative poetry continued here and there to be written. Panyasis, the kinsman of Herodotus, is one of those stepping-stones. About the time of the Persian wars he composed his *Heracleia,* a poem of some 9000 lines, and therefore of the epic magnitude, dealing with certain among the adventures of Heracles; it may or may not have been a supplement to the earlier *Heracleia* of the Rhodian Peisander, one of the later cyclists whose date is about the middle of the seventh century. Both were classed among the epic poets in Alexandrian lists. So was another poet of about a century later, Antimachus of Claros, whose *Thebaid,* a poem of enormous length, is said to have won the praise of Plato when he heard it read, and later served as a model to Statius. Another *Thebaid,* which, however, seems to have been a chronicle rather than an epic, was written by Antagoras of Rhodes, a friend of Aratus, and belonging therefore to the age of Callimachus. These names, and others even more shadowy, all belong to a single area, the south-western corner of Asia Minor and the outlying islands. They suggest that in that corner of the Greek world at least, the tradition and practice of long narrative poems was continuous, and that when Apollonius left Alexandria for Rhodes it was not merely a self-imposed exile, but a movement into a more sympathetic environment. He did not only gather a circle there, he found one already existing; and he gave that poetical school a new direction, and even, we might say, a new vitality. The romantic epic, as it finally left his hands, had become a recognised and in some sense a classical form of poetry. To gain that position, it had to make large compromises; and compromise in poetry, as in all art, brings with it the inevitable consequence of mediocrity. Apollonius had not the controlling genius required to merge and fuse the newer with the older elements; that was left for his immortal pupil. Both had that infinite capacity for taking pains which has so often been confounded with genius; but Virgil had genius as well.

In one thing at least Apollonius was happy, and that was in his choice of subject. The Quest of the Golden Fleece is a story of imperishable interest and charm, second only perhaps in that respect to the story of the Odyssey, superior even to the story of the Odyssey in its rounded completeness. It combines in the happiest way the two great motives of love and adventure: it is rich in episodic matter, and yet on its main lines moves forward, from the coming of Jason to Iolcos down to his triumphant return, with a single and accumulating interest. Its danger lies in its richness; the wealth of detail is so great that without high architectonic power the structure falls to pieces and the main interest becomes smothered. This power, one of the greatest and most indispensable in poetry, Apollonius did not possess. In the *Argonautica* we feel that the poet is trying to do several things at once, and that he has not the constructive power to give them organic unity, has not the imaginative ardour to fuse them in a single controlling movement. He has neither the power of composing on a great scale such as would be needed to handle and incorporate the whole of his material, nor the strength of mind and clearsightedness of judgment to discard what only interfered with the unity and blurred the tone of what he might have chosen for the scope of a single romance. To compare him with Virgil is instructive, but as regards this particular point partly irrelevant, for Virgil's object was different; yet so far as the objects of the two poets coincide, we can clearly see in the earlier poet the fumbling of a scholar, in the later the secure handling of a master. But if we compare the *Argonautica* with the English treatment of the same story in the *Life and Death of Jason*, we see at once that where Apollonius fails is in lack of the true narrative gift—that exceedingly rare and exceedingly precious quality—and in lack of constructive or architectural power. In that last quality, throughout his whole work, Morris is faultless. Apollonius, like many other eminent poets, did not possess it, did not at least possess it effectively. He was capable of beautiful episodes, exquisite similes and descriptive passages; he brought into poetry, here and there, a romantic touch which was new and his own; but he had not the sustained grasp and range required to produce a great poem. Hence it is that he so often produces the impression of not knowing clearly what he would be at. He is like those artists whose drawing is fundamentally wrong, and who labour on in a sort of half-unconscious hope that it will come right in the painting. But it does not.

The beauty of the detail in the *Argonautica* is often beyond praise. It is not surprising that critics, whose eye is necessarily fixed on detail, have sometimes been misled into thinking that it is the detail that matters, and that ornament need not be judged by its relation to structure. It was a desperate saying of one of these, which need not be taken too seriously, that Apollonius was better than Virgil. Perhaps the merits of Apollonius had to be over-emphasised to redress the balance of the orthodox criticism, contemptuous because it was undiscriminating. The way in which Conington handles the matter in his preface to the Aeneid gives sufficient illustration of what I mean. The substance of his attack is that the *Argonautica* is not epic. To this charge, put baldly thus, the answer is that it is not epic because it was not meant to be epic; it is romance. Its real failure is that the author had not the genius or courage to shake himself clear of the epic tradition, and to launch himself on romance boldly. But to do that would have required a genius of the first rank; and if he had done it, it would have meant, in the full sense, not a revolt but a revolution. Still more unjust is the charge, also made by Conington, that the language of the *Argonautica* is, "though sometimes graceful and ingenious, the mere jargon of a grammarian seeking to revive a mode of speech of which he had no living appreciation." If we approach Alexandrian poetry with this preconception, we shall never even begin to understand it. The sneer of Callimachus—ἄλλος ἔχει,[1] "done already"—not only might be turned against Callimachus himself with equal justice, but is one of those facile and irrelevant criticisms that can be made against nearly all poetry, and generally are in fact made against any new poet. *Nullumst iam dictum quod non dictum sit prius:* yes, and

[1] *Anth. Pal.*, xii. 43.

what then? It is the essential glory of poetry that it perpetually reincarnates what is as old as the beginnings of the heaven and earth. What Callimachus really complained of in the young school, what really shocked and irritated him, was not that Apollonius was an imitator, but that he was an innovator. New poetry is generally regarded by the older poets with alarm; themselves innovators in their time, they are subject to the delusion (shared by them with politicians, and indeed with mankind generally) that they have reached finality, and that the further progress of poetry means decadence, and is either arrogant or vulgar, or both. Coleridge thought Tennyson wrote *Mariana* and *Oenone* and the *Hesperides* "without very well understanding what metre is." Tennyson could not see any merit in "little Swinburne." So the story runs from one generation to another. Callimachus' words, "I hate the cyclic poem"—ἐχθαίρω τὸ ποίημα τὸ κυκλικόν—if, as appears, they were levelled expressly at Apollonius, were an attack not on his Homericism but on that new and specifically romantic treatment of which Apollonius was the standard-bearer, and which to Callimachus seemed vulgarity. In a vicious but not remarkaby clever couplet, Apollonius retorted by calling Callimachus a "wooden head"—ξυλινὸς νοῦς.[1] So too Swinburne replied to Tennyson's "poisonous honey" with something about "treacle" which was not calculated to make things smoother. But these amenities of literary men are not very edifying reading.

[1] *Anth. Pal.*, xi. 275.

The fame of Apollonius and the lasting charm of his poem rest on the third book. One would like to believe that it represents the core of the poem as he originally conceived and wrote it. It stands out from the rest, not so much by greater beauty of detail as by greater unity of tone and radiance of colour. It is the spirit of romance finding, however imperfectly, a continuous voice; and that voice is the more strange and fascinating because it is mingled with notes of the new realism which Apollonius, like the whole of the earlier Alexandrians, was feeling after. To this central part of the poem the first and second books are in effect a prologue lengthened out to tediousness, and the fourth an epilogue which only escapes tediousness by the heroic remedy of stopping abruptly before the story reaches its end. Comparisons are not only odious but generally misleading; yet it would not be wholly misleading to compare with the whole poem, in its poetical effect, an Aeneid consisting of the first, third, and fifth books only, if the third book remained, according to Virgil's original plan, a direct narrative, and if the fifth were extended a little so as to include part of the seventh and bring the Trojans into Latium. Evidently such a poem would have no unity and no balance; it would be constructively, and therefore essentially, wrong; and this would be quite independent of whether the treatment were definable generally as classical or as romantic. It might be either, or both; but it would be simply wrong. We should read it for the sake of the Fourth Book (the third, that is to say, of the four which would compose the poem) and for the detached beauties of the other three. And that is in effect what we do with the *Argonautica*.

Romance, in the sense in which I have been speaking of it, may bear two meanings. There is the romance of situation, and the romance of incident. The distinction corresponds roughly to the distinction between the two leading motives of romantic poetry, love and adventure. It is only when they are combined that the new form of poetry—the romantic epic as we call it, for want of a better term—succeeds fully in doing what it means to do. The term romantic epic is of course a clumsy one; the thing it describes is neither an epic nor a romance. In the *Argonautica*, as also in the Aeneid, there are three distinguishable threads: the epic thread, that of a single heroic action; the chronicle thread, that of a series of historical or quasi-historical events, not in themselves possessing unity; and the romance thread proper, that of a passionate situation. Virgil wove, or rather fused, the three into a single magnificent texture. In the *Argonautica* they lie side by side, detachably: they even to a certain extent jar upon one another. Throughout the progress of the narrative one feels Apollonius consciously wavering between two things which are really incompatible, the epic subject of the achievement of the Quest of the Golden Fleece by Jason, and the chronicle-romance of the Argonauts. For the former of these two he was unequal and probably unwilling; he did not set out to write an epic, but a new kind of poem differing from the epic.

Yet he could not let himself go upon the latter. Every now and then he pulls himself up with an obvious jerk to get back into the main subject; the effect is awkward, and according to the reader's mood either distressing or ludicrous. "But why need I tell out in full the story of Aethalides?" (i. 648). "Of these things I will speak no further" (i. 919), when they have put in on the island of Electra. "If I must needs recount this also in detail under the dictation of the Muses" is his excuse, which only makes things worse, when (ii. 844) he cannot bring himself to cut out a piece of irrelevant antiquarianism, suited for a chronicle but not for a poem, and even in a chronicle rather an intercalated note than anything properly belonging to the chronicle itself. Or once more, and this time with a painfully ludicrous effect (i. 1220), where he has, in the episode of Hylas and Heracles, got entangled in a digression from a digression, and breaks it short with the fatuous reflection ἀλλὰ τὰ μὲν τηλοῦ κεν ἀποπλάγξειεν ἀοιδῆς—"this however will lead me far astray from my poem." It will; but there is no need to say so, or to get to a point where it has to be said. It suggests, it even provokes, satirical treatment: *But why should I encumber you with histories of Matthew Coo?—Let Matthew Coo at once take wing: 'tis not of him I'm going to sing.* Here and there, in the first two books, one almost can hear Apollonius murmuring to himself another verse of the same ballad—

> Come, come, I say, we've had enough
> Of this absurd disjointed stuff;
> Let us get on to that affair.

What is it that redeems these two books, giving as they do in this way the effect of an unwilling and badly planned abridgment, and yet even in their abridged form taking up nearly half the poem in bringing us to the period where the real central action begins? What enables us to read them with an interest that never quite fails and sometimes rises into keen enjoyment? The answer is not single. Partly it is the uniform grace and finish of the language, that exquisite Greek which works in precious stone where other languages have to make what they can of ordinary pebbles. Partly it is the inherent and unsurpassed interest of the story as a mere chronicle of adventures. Partly it is the pieces of lovely detail, descriptions and comparisons and, less often, reflections, which make the *Argonautica* so quotable, and make it seem in quotations so much finer than it actually is. Partly too it is because we know that the Medea and Jason story is on its way, and look forward to it so keenly that we would not hurry on to it, but rather welcome than deprecate the successive delays through which we are brought up towards it.

It would take too long now to analyse however briefly the contents of these two books; but it would be only through such an analysis that one could bring out the immense pains taken by Apollonius to avoid the monotony of a chronicle poem, his resourcefulness in varying the treatment and interspersing it with fresh motives, and yet the futility in the upshot of all that labour and resource, because the bones of the poem are wrong, its organic structure faulty. Structurally, as a matter of composition, the *Argonautica* is judged and condemned on the first two hundred and fifty lines. It is one of the qualities of all really great poetry that it strikes its note, sets its scene, gets its action arranged and its movement determined, at once and with complete certainty. Great artists know this by instinct; and where we can trace their handling and construction through successive works, we can see them lay more and more stress on this point, and sacrifice more and more to make it, knowing well that it is worth more than they can possibly spend on it. Here it is that Apollonius goes hopelessly wrong; and this is not from any vicious convention common to him with the Alexandrian school, nor yet from any principle inherent in his own new method; it is simply from his being an inferior artist. These first two hundred and fifty lines, if compared, not to say with the supreme art of Homer or Virgil or Milton, but with the sound workmanlike art of quite secondary poets, are simply deplorable. First there is the formal invocation; this had to be there, and it is a mere matter of four lines. Then follows a sort of tragic prologue, reproducing quite unnecessarily one of the worst concessions that the Attic drama made in its decline to what were, or were thought to be, the exigencies of the theatre; then more than two hundred lines of a catalogue, a dangerous thing anywhere and requiring immense skill to lift into the movement of a poem, but here perfectly benumbing and lowering in its effect; "it strikes a man more dead," in Touchstone's phrase, "than a great reckoning in a little room." "Truly," Touchstone goes on, "I would the gods had made thee poetical." Only at the two hundred and thirty-fourth line does Apollonius at last get launched on his poem, and even then it creaks and groans before it begins to move. It is symptomatic that the first piece of deliberate ornament in it—and it is the kind of ornament which he elsewhere uses most beautifully—is awkward and inappropriate. The grief of the mother of one of the Argonauts as she parts from her son is compared, in an elaborate simile, to the grief of a stepmothered girl sobbing on the bosom of her old nurse—a simile that illustrates nothing, either by likeness or by contrast. This is not so much failure in poetical power—though it is that too—as failure in ordinary intelligence.

To a certain degree, indeed, this same failure in intelligence pervades the whole poem as regards the application and setting of ornament. Many of Virgil's most exquisite passages of ornament are taken bodily from Apollonius; we shall uniformly find that he gives them a new and heightened value, the value that ornament takes by being in the right place. One or two instances will bring this out very clearly. In a very beautiful passage in the fourth book of the *Argonautica*, when the Argonauts have been toiling for many days waterless through the terrible Libyan desert, the night-wind brings to them a mysterious sound as of steps moving through the sand. Five of them start out to see; and Lynceus the keen-sighted "now thought he saw Heracles alone, far away over the endless land, in such wise as a man sees or thinks he sees the new moon through a mist." The simile is beautiful in itself, but not specially appropriate; there was nothing ghostly about Heracles: the ornament is otiose, for it adds no light and gives no thrill. Virgil took it and transfigured it, in the immortal passage where Aeneas sees the faint ghost of Dido moving through the myrtle-forest in the dusk of the underworld. Or take another instance almost as striking. As Medea and Jason "at the hour," says Apollonius, "when huntsmen were shaking sleep from their eyes," a little before dawn, approach the dragon that guards the Golden Fleece, he utters a dreadful hissing scream: "so that the grove and the long banks of the river echoed strangely around: even they heard it who dwelt in the Colchian land far from Aea . . . and women still in childbed started up and cast their arms in agony about their infants who were sleeping in the fold of their arms and leapt at the scream." Here again Virgil copies Apollonius in the splendid description of the trumpet-blast of Allecto in the seventh Aeneid (ll. 514–518) that roars through all the deep woodland and is heard by the water of Nar and the springs of Velinus, and frightened mothers clasp their children close to their breast. The beauty of the picture in Apollonius, in spite of his breaking it up by three lines of quite irrelevant geography, is great; yet somehow it fails to stir us, and when we ask ourselves why, the reason is at once clear. Nothing came of this dreadful sound; it is heard, he tells us, all over Colchis, and yet it does not awaken Aeetes or a soul in the city. It is the mere painted picture

R

of a sound; there is no thought, no shaping imagination, behind the ornament.

It is needless to multiply instances; and one turns gladly from these ambitious failures—which yet, like the large ambitious failure of the whole poem itself, are the preludes of a new and great poetry, the clouded lights not of evening but of dawn—to other passages where a true and exquisite feeling for nature is expressed in language all but faultless. Such are the descriptions — pictures alike pure in line and lovely in colour—of dawn kindling on the highest crags of Pelion, and far below, the soft heaving of the morning seas (i. 519–521); and again, daylight breaking high up in the sky, and the grey roads becoming luminous, and the level dew-drenched meadows glimmering to the dawn (i. 1280–82); and once more, full morning, with the shredded night flying out of the sky, and the island beaches and dewy field-tracks laughing back to the sunrise (iv. 1170–72); or of the afternoon shadows, when the day has ceased to stand still, slowly advancing over the cornfields at the foot of the cliffs (i. 450–452); or the picture, sharply etched and vivid, of the wind rising at night after a heavy snowfall and blowing the clouds away, so that the whole sky is a clear blackness crowded with glittering stars (iii. 1359–1362). The quick sensitiveness and skill of handling shown in passages like these (and there are many) sometimes lends itself to weird effects, unique in ancient poetry and reminding one of the great modern romanticists. Such is the remarkable description of the Black Country of the

Chalybes, that sent its steel over the Mediterranean world (ii. 1002–8); an ancient Pittsburg or Middlesborough, a land which has to import all its food, without tillage or pasturage, where labour in the mines and furnaces goes on continuously by night and day under an unlifting canopy of smoke and amid a lurid glow of flame. As unique as that picture, and even more startling, is another, further on in the same book (ii. 1247–1259), where for once at least daring imagination has succeeded triumphantly in making weird and awful what might easily have been merely grotesque or silly. That is the sight that the Argonauts have of the eagle of Prometheus, rushing overhead like some great aeroplane, the wind of its pinions laying all their sails aback as it passed overhead with incredible speed; "strange-shaped, not like a bird, but the feathers pulsed like oars"; it rose out of the evening dusk, hurtled over them, and melted into the dusk again, and a little after came a great cry from the mountain, that rang through all the heaven. There had been nothing so daring since Aeschylus: it must needs make us wonder what Apollonius could have done if he had trusted the romantic impulse and let himself go.

As it was, the romantic impulse works in him intermittently; it is timorous and discontinuous; partly because tradition was too strong for him, partly because of another impulse which crossed and thwarted it. This was the impulse towards realism which he shared with the whole of the Alexandrians, and which meant both in him and them, as I have again and again insisted, the attempt to get poetry back into an organic relation with life. If I seem to repeat this too often, it is because the tendency to forget it is so great; and if we forget this we shall never understand the Alexandrians, and which is more important still, never understand what the progress of poetry actually was on its movement from Hellas to the West.

But Apollonius differed from the older Alexandrians—and from his own successors, so far as we know anything about these, as well—in being essentially and primarily a romanticist. His divergences into realism are generally not very happy; his heart is not in them, and they sound out of tone; his voice goes flat, he becomes here and there almost vulgar. His worst failure in the whole poem is where, in the episode of the visit of Hera and Athena to Aphrodite at the beginning of Book III., he tries to galvanise the obsolete epic machinery into new life by introducing into it a sort of bourgeois detail. The description of Aphrodite "sitting on a chair on castors opposite the door" and hastily putting up her half-finished plaits into a coil with both her hands that she may attend to her visitors, brings us into the atmosphere of the *Adoniazusae*; and Theocritus would have done it exquisitely; where it comes, it is dreadful. On the other hand, the romantic passages in Apollonius, even when irrelevant, are always beautiful in themselves: they are sometimes in the poem rather than of it, but they hang in it like jewels. Such for instance is the strange little vignette of the girl watching the full moon rise from her bedchamber, and catching the moonlight in the folds of her thin smock (iv. 167–9)—singularly like, though with a difference, the scene of Madeline's undressing in the *Eve of St. Agnes,* familiar not only in the poem but in the visual interpretation of it given by Millais in one of the most beautiful and romantic of his pictures. Such again, but here with a power and amplitude that raises it to the height of classical romance, is the description of the world seen from the gates of heaven, outside of the celestial palace with its encompassing gardens and orchards. It comes with the more startling effect at the end of an episode where Apollonius had been at his unhappiest, that of the scene among the three goddesses, where the epic machinery is used mechanically and without conviction, and the attempt to give it new vitality by rendering it with a modern colour and surroundings only makes it silly without making it romantic. All of a sudden at the end of this episode come the wonderful lines (iii. 160–166) with their vision, as clear as in a picture, of the whole of middle-earth as it lies under the cope of heaven. It half anticipates the magnificent passage in *Sigurd the Volsung* where Sigurd and Brynhild look down from the head of Hindfell upon the kingdoms of the world. It is possible even that in Morris's mind there may have been some recollection and suggestion surviving and renewing itself from the years long before when he had read Apollonius for his own poem of the Golden Fleece. But if so, we must notice once again how the great poet gives a wholly new value to what he takes from an inferior predecessor. The passage in *Sigurd* comes exactly where it ought, and is exactly right, exactly in tone:—

For far away beneath them lie the kingdoms of the earth,
And the garths of men-folk's dwellings and the streams that water them,
And the rich and plenteous acres, and the silver ocean's hem,
And the woodland wastes and the mountains, and all that holdeth all;
The house and the ship and the island, the loom and the mine and the stall,
The beds of bane and healing, the crafts that slay and save,
The temple of God and the Doom-ring, the cradle and the grave.

The lines of Apollonius, which are in some sense the germ or original of these, are as follows:—

—ἔνθεν δὲ καταιβάτις ἐστὶ κέλευθος
οὐρανίη, δοιὼ δὲ πόλοι ἀνέχουσι κάρηνα
οὐρέων ἠλιβάτων, κορυφαὶ χθονός, ἧχί τ' ἀερθεὶς
ἠέλιος πρώτῃσιν ἐρεύθεται ἀκτίνεσσιν.
νειόθι δ' ἄλλοτε γαῖα φερέσβιος ἄστεά τ' ἀνδρῶν
φαίνετο καὶ ποταμῶν ἱεροὶ ῥόοι, ἄλλοτε δ' αὖτε
ἄκριες, ἀμφὶ δὲ πόντος ἀν' αἰθέρα πολλὸν ἰόντι.

I do not add any English rendering of the lines, for their clear beauty and imaginative quality depend so largely on their actual form and music that a translation would be blurred and disappointing. They reach perhaps the highest point of imaginative value touched in the *Argonautica*.

And in one way they come where they do appropriately; for they stand at the opening of the Jason and Medea episode in which the romanticism of Apollonius is concentrated, and for the sake of which, one might say, the whole poem exists. All critics are agreed as to the grace and charm, the delicate sensibility and romantic beauty of this famous episode. Virgil here did not better his model; he diverged from it and made it into something different, something greater indeed, deeper and more majestic, but hardly more beautiful. In both cases it is interesting to notice how the poet has lavished his art on the portraiture of the woman and left the man to shift for himself, a little inadequate, a little unsympathetic. In both cases the art proved greater than the artist. We feel with Jason something of the same impatience that we feel with Aeneas. Both keep their heads, both seem cold and selfish in contrast with the burning surrender of Medea and Dido. Aeneas indeed is a man of sorrows, bearing on his shoulders not only the destinies of a future empire, but the burden of a wrecked life: he is "widower Aeneas," as Sebastian calls him in *The Tempest*, in a passage remarkable as being the single piece of Virgilian criticism ever made by a poet as great as Virgil; and his *neque haec in foedera veni* comes from him with a solemnity that makes one feel and understand how to him love might be a little thing. "In me thou see'st the glowing of such fire that on the ashes of his youth doth lie." For Jason, in all the splendour of his brilliant youth, we can feel less sympathy; nor does Apollonius leave us sure whether his portraiture shows some bluntness of feeling or is a piece of delicate though tragic psychology. To us at all events the later tragedy casts its shadow dark over the love-scene in Colchis. But that tragedy is outside of the scheme of the *Argonautica*, and ignored in it; unless indeed there be just one fugitive veiled allusion to it in the passage where Jason, pleading with Medea, cites to her the example of Ariadne, as though suggesting indirectly, to himself or to us, that Ariadne was not the only princess who would save her lover's life, and give everything to him, only to be abandoned.

Apart from this, the whole episode is on a high, almost on the highest level. The splendid description of night with which it opens is one of the passages copied by Virgil in the well-known and magical lines of the fourth Aeneid beginning *Nox erat et placidum carpebant fessa soporem,* and concentrated by him as usual to a greater splendour, though for once not raised to a higher or more apt beauty, and scarcely conveying with the same overpowering effect the sense of vast stillness enveloping alike those who were asleep and those who were awake. "Night drew her shadow across the world: sailors at sea gazed from their ships at Helice and the stars in Orion; wayfarer and watchman at the gates longed to be asleep; the mother whose children were dead lay wrapped in heavy slumber; not a dog barked in the town, not a footfall sounded in the street: silence filled the blackness of the night": *at non infelix animi*—all this vast weight of silence surrounded the sleepless passion of one heart. Praise of this would be almost an impertinence; or of the passage later (one of the most moving in poetry), where Medea recoils from the thought of killing herself as she thinks of all the joys of living, and of her own childhood, "and the sun was sweeter to behold"; or of the meeting of the lovers in the temple: τὼ δ' ἄνεῳ καὶ ἄναυδοι—both speechless and silent, "like trees that stand silent side by side in the stillness, till a breath of wind comes to rustle them, and then they murmur endlessly, as these two were soon to find voice under the breath of Love."

These and others are notable passages; but almost throughout, Apollonius here is at his best; he has found romance, he has created the romantic treatment. And as long as this impulse lasts and carries him on, the poem continues to move in a higher air. The return of the Argonauts, up to the point at which they reach the land of the Phaeacians and the marriage of Jason and Medea is consummated, is, as romantic narrative, on a level not unworthy of the central episode. He is no longer hampered by that Alexandrian tradition of the chronicle-narrative which had encrusted the outward voyage of Books I. and II. with such unmanageable masses of material—history, geography, archaeology. He can let his imagination go. The result may be a little too like an Arabian Tale, a voyage of Sindbad or Judar; but it is full of spirit and excitement and the sense of boundless strangeness; not the less so that the geography is perfectly delirious. The obstinate belief in some undiscoverable North-West passage is mixed up to such a degree with fragmentary information from misunderstood maps that we seem to be in a wild dream. Rivers flow both ways indifferently, and communicate with one another through a maze of channels. The Rhine and the Danube, the Po and the Adige and the Rhone, are all faintly identifiable in this strange network of navigable streams and lakes, fed from springs "in a land far away, where are the portals and the habitations of Night." When at last the Argonauts get past these into the Odyssean wonderland, and come to the palace of Circe and the island of the Sirens and the court of Phaeacia, it is almost like a return to real life.

But the romantic impulse which had carried on the poem so far does not last out; and Apollonius has to pay the price for his want of constructive power, for the failure of a guiding plan. His imagination rapidly ebbs away, and the poem dwindles and stops. At the end the method of chronicle-romance is resumed, but he has no heart in it; "there were no further adventures," he ends, "until they reached home." Never poem had a flatter or lamer ending.

The point at which the *Argonautica* ends corresponds pretty nearly to the end of the fourteenth book of the *Life and Death of Jason;* and up to this point the two poems are approximately on the same scale: 6000 lines of Apollonius as against 7500 of Morris. But that Morris, or that any poet with the instinct for narrative and the gift of construction, would have stopped at this point is unimaginable. Indeed, few studies in poetry could be either more interesting or more instructive than to lay these two poems side by side and observe the differences of handling, alike in the main construction and the detailed evolution of the poem; to consider likewise how far the failure of

Apollonius is due to his having (like all explorers in the realm of poetry) no very clear conception of what he meant to do, how far to mere weakness, and how far to the hampering and overpowering classical tradition. This there is no opportunity to do here; but one point of special interest may be mentioned: that is, the method in which the romantic epic brings itself into relation with the lyric. Both poems include songs of Orpheus to his fellow-Argonauts. In Apollonius there are two: the one, a song of the creation of the world and a theogony, sung by him on the Argo at the beginning of its outward voyage; the other, a hymn to Apollo, sung by him at a sacrifice made by the Argonauts on the sacred island of Thynias in the Euxine. Both of them, it may be noted in passing, were taken up and used by Virgil—the former in the song of Silenus in the sixth Eclogue, the latter in the hymn to Hercules in the eighth Aeneid; in the latter, Virgil has copied the adroit device by which, through a change from the third person into the second, the narrative slides into a direct lyric; in the former, both Apollonius and Virgil use the form of the indirect or reported lyric (*namque canebat uti*—ἤειδεν δ' ὡς), a rather dangerous experiment, with great skill and beauty. Morris, with a longer tradition behind him, was able to adopt a freer handling. The lyrics in *Jason*—among the loveliest in English—are interposed in the narrative, and the difference further emphasised by a change of metre. Five of them are sung by Orpheus; and in each case they give the momentary uplifting and concentration of emotion, they make the sliding chain of the narrative blaze into a jewel. The greater freedom of modern romance allows a poet to do many things which in its beginnings, when it was still tentative and still hampered by the full weight of the classical tradition, seemed impossible. On this particular point it is noticeable that Chaucer did not think fit to vary the metre for the lyrics in *Troilus and Creseide.* The more nearly a romance approaches the epic scale and movement, the more necessary it would seem to be that it should preserve a continuous metrical texture. The intercalated lyric seems only to find its place in a narrative poem which does not attempt to rise beyond romance. If we study the practice of Morris we shall see that he uses the interposed lyric less and less in the *Earthly Paradise* as his mind, under the influence of the great Icelandic epic, moves towards the epic handling and environment of life. In his own epic of *Sigurd the Volsung* he discards it altogether. The song of Orpheus in the first book of the *Argonautica* (that describing the Creation and the birth of the Gods) stands midway in method between the frankly intercalated lyrics of the *Jason* and the song of Gunnar in Atli's worm-pit, where the subject is the same as that of Orpheus, but the lyric is welded into the structure of the epic, and is no longer episodic ornament (however beautiful and apt) but organic.

We must never forget with Apollonius that he was attempting something quite new; he was not only an innovator but a beginner, working experimentally and tentatively towards an end not distinctly seen—an end which could not well be distinctly seen until it should have been actually reached. His failure counts as the equivalent of many successes; for he opened a new door to poetry, though he did not succeed in passing fully through it. The marriage of epic and romance was effected by him, though it was, like the marriage of Jason and Medea in his own poem, effected hastily and prematurely. It had to be done then somehow if it was to be done at all. Those who have read the *Argonautica* cannot fail to remember the passage, one of the finest in the whole poem alike for dramatic value and for beauty of treatment. The Colchian host have come to Phaeacia to claim back the fugitive. Medea throws herself in the most touching way on the mercy of Queen Arete, who pleads for her with Alcinous. He gives his judgment: "If she be yet a maid, they shall carry her back to her father; but if she share a husband's bed I will not separate her from her lord, nor if she carry a child within her womb will I give her up to her enemies." Arete at once sends word to Jason and Medea; and they are hastily married with "such maimed rites" as the sudden occasion allows; Orpheus sings before the bridal bower, but round it all night are the Argonaut spearmen, guarding it from the Colchians. "Not now was the hero, the son of Aeson, desirous to complete his marriage, but in the halls of his father when he should return to Iolcos; and Medea also was of like mind with him"—notice how the two are thought of still as separate and independent—"yet necessity drove them to marry there and then. So is it that we tribes of harassed mankind never plant a foot full on delight, but ever some sharp pang comes alongside of our felicities." In such haste as this, and with such allayed and shaken happiness, the union of epic and romance was effected by Apollonius. But even so the two were united, and became one flesh.

For a time the marriage was without issue; at least so it would appear. Apollonius did not give a new course to Greek poetry; for Greek poetry was beginning to fade away and die. Such later attempts as were made in the new manner have disappeared. The *Messeniaca* of Rhianus, a younger contemporary, only known now by a few imponderable fragments, seems to have treated the chronicle-epic with some approach to the romantic manner. I only mention it here because its story, like that of the *Argonautica*, was one of those selected by Morris when he first conceived the scheme of the *Earthly Paradise*. Both were written by him in the same year, and neither appeared in the *Earthly Paradise* as it took its final shape. The *Life and Death of Jason* outgrew its first scope and became a separate work; the *Aristomenes* was never finished and remains still unpublished. Morris had become dissatisfied with it, feeling the subject was too historical for the free play of the romantic method. Probably this was the case with the poem of Rhianus also. The romance in later Greek literature divorced itself from the poetical forms of the epic and took to prose as the vehicle for imaginative narrative combining the interests of love and adventure. The true successors of Apollonius are on the one hand the romantic novel, on the other, Virgil the romanticist.

In studying Theocritus we have had occasion again and again to notice his close poetical affinity with Tennyson. In the early sixties the great English idylist had come to a pause in his production of poetry; the idyllic method was for the time exhausted. It was then that Morris, like Apollonius, but with a higher genius and freer movement, reinstated the long narrative poem, the romance or romantic epic, in the poetry of England. Like Apollonius, he hardly founded a school; for his genius was in this as in other matters unique and untransmissible. The differences are larger and more important than the analogies between the two; yet the analogies are striking and suggestive. But the history of poetry never repeats itself in its progress; and this is just one of the reasons why poetry is, in its progress no less than in its achieved results, so endlessly fascinating.

When we speak of the poetry of any age, or of any poet, as artificial, we perhaps hardly realise how fragile and how artificial all poetry is. Its abiding life is not here. It never continues in one stay. Its embodiments are transitory, and its light has no sooner touched any one point than it begins, in the same movement, to glide off it. The images of perfection which it successively condenses from the flying vapours of the world have only a transcendental permanence; we can see them forming and melting in one and the same breath. In the earlier Alexandrian poetry we can just catch a last condensation of the Hellenic genius, a gleam of the old light before the chill came with sunset and the eastward-wheeling earth drove the shadow up the wall. With the later poets of the school the light gradually and surely disappears. Morning was kindling elsewhere, and at last they were left with the night. *Sie waren längst gestorben, und wussten es selber kaum.*

To conclude, I announce what comes after me.

I have pressed through in my own right,
I have sung the body and the soul, war and peace have I sung, and
the songs of life and death,
And the songs of birth, and shown that there are many births.

So I pass, a little time vocal, visible, contrary,
Afterward a melodious echo, passionately bent for (death making
me really undying),
The best of me then when no longer visible, for toward that I have
been incessantly repairing.

What is there more, that I lag and pause and crouch extended with
unshut mouth?
Is there a single final farewell?

Remember my words, I may again return,
I love you, I depart from materials,
I am as one disembodied, triumphant, dead.

Printed by Ballantyne, Hanson & Co.
Edinburgh & London

Classical Literature, Translations, &c.

THE WORLD OF HOMER. By ANDREW LANG. 8vo, 6s. 6d. net.

HOMER AND HIS AGE. By ANDREW LANG. With 8 Illustrations. 8vo, 12s. 6d. net.

TALES OF TROY AND GREECE. By ANDREW LANG. Crown 8vo, 4s. 6d. net.

HOMER'S ODYSSEY. Done into English Verse. By WILLIAM MORRIS. Crown 8vo, 5s. net.

THE GROWTH OF THE HOMERIC POEMS. By G. WILKINS. 8vo, 6s.

HANDBOOK OF HOMERIC STUDY. By HENRY BROWNE, S.J., M.A. With 22 Plates. Crown 8vo, 6s. net.

HELLENICA. A Collection of Essays on Greek Poetry, Philosophy, History, and Religion. Edited by EVELYN ABBOTT, M.A., LL.D. Crown 8vo, 7s. 6d.

THE EUMENIDES OF ÆSCHYLUS. With Metrical English Translation. By J. F. DAVIES. 8vo, 7s.

THE ACHARNIANS OF ARISTOPHANES. Translated into English Verse. By R. Y. TYRRELL. Crown 8vo, 1s.

SOPHOCLES. Translated into English Verse. By ROBERT WHITELAW, M.A., Assistant Master in Rugby School. Crown 8vo, 8s. 6d.

RELIGION IN GREEK LITERATURE. By the Rev. LEWIS CAMPBELL, M.A., LL.D. 8vo, 15s.

SELECT EPIGRAMS FROM THE GREEK ANTHOLOGY. Edited, with Revised Text, Translation, Introduction, and Notes, by J. W. MACKAIL, M.A., LL.D. 8vo, 14s. net.

POCKET EDITION, 2 vols. (Greek Text, 1 vol.) (English Translation, 1 vol.), fcap. 8vo, gilt top, each 2s. net; leather, 3s. net.

CHARICLES; or, Illustrations of the Private Life of the Ancient Greeks. By W. A. BECKER. Translated by the Rev. F. METCALFE, B.D. With Notes and Excursuses. With 26 Illustrations. Crown 8vo, 3s. 6d.

DUBLIN TRANSLATIONS INTO GREEK AND LATIN VERSE. Edited by R. Y. TYRRELL. 8vo, 6s.

LONGMANS, GREEN AND CO.
LONDON, NEW YORK, BOMBAY, AND CALCUTTA

Classical Literature, Translations, &c.

THE PHARSALIA OF LUCAN. Translated into Blank Verse by Sir EDWARD RIDLEY, sometime Fellow of All Souls College, Oxford, one of the Judges of the High Court of Justice. 8vo, 14s.

CICERO'S CORRESPONDENCE. By R. Y. TYRRELL. Vols. I., II., III., 8vo, each 12s. Vol. IV., 15s. Vol. V., 14s. Vol. VI., 12s. Vol. VII., Index, 7s. 6d.

GALLUS; or, Roman Scenes in the Time of Augustus. By W. A. BECKER. Translated by the Rev. F. METCALFE, B.D. With Notes and Excursuses. With 26 Illustrations. Crown 8vo, 3s. 6d.

HORAE LATINAE: Studies in Synonyms and Syntax. By the late ROBERT OGILVIE, M.A., LL.D., H.M. Chief Inspector of Schools for Scotland. Edited by ALEXANDER SOUTER, M.A. 8vo, gilt top, 12s. 6d. net.

A DICTIONARY OF ROMAN AND GREEK ANTIQUITIES. By A. RICH, B.A. With 2000 Illustrations. Crown 8vo, 6s. net.

VIRGIL.

THE POEMS OF VIRGIL. Translated into English Prose. By JOHN CONINGTON. Crown 8vo, gilt top, 6s.

THE ÆNEID OF VIRGIL. Translated into English Verse. By JOHN CONINGTON. Crown 8vo, 2s. 6d. net.

THE ÆNEIDS OF VIRGIL. Done into English Verse. By WILLIAM MORRIS. Crown 8vo, 5s. net.

THE ÆNEID OF VIRGIL, freely translated into English Blank Verse. By W. J. THORNHILL. Crown 8vo, 7s. 6d.

THE ÆNEID OF VIRGIL. Translated into English Verse. By JAMES RHOADES. Crown 8vo.

Books I.–VI., 2s. net; Books VII.–XII., 2s. net; complete in One Volume, 3s. 6d. net.

THE ECLOGUES AND GEORGICS OF VIRGIL. Translated from the Latin into English Prose. By J. W. MACKAIL, Fellow of Balliol College, Oxford. Square 16mo, 5s.

HARVARD STUDIES IN CLASSICAL PHILOLOGY. Edited by a Committee of the Classical Instructors of Harvard University. Volumes XI. to XX. 8vo, 6s. 6d. net each.

SOME PASSAGES IN THE EARLY HISTORY OF CLASSICAL LEARNING IN IRELAND. An Address delivered at the Inaugural Meeting of the Trinity College Classical Society. By the Right Hon. Mr. JUSTICE MADDEN, M.A., Hon. LL.D., Vice-Chancellor of the University of Dublin. Crown 8vo, 2s. 6d. net.

LONGMANS, GREEN AND CO.
LONDON, NEW YORK, BOMBAY, AND CALCUTTA